T0115040

SENSORY INTEGRATION PLUS

A FAMILY'S STORY OF LOVE AND LEARNING

WENDY VANN MS, LPC

BALBOA.
PRESS

A DIVISION OF HAY HOUSE

Author Credits: Licensed Professional Counselor

Balboa Press books may be ordered through booksellers or by contacting:

Balboa Press
A Division of Hay House
1663 Liberty Drive
Bloomington, IN 47403
www.balboapress.com
1 (877) 407-4847

Print information available on the last page.

ISBN: 978-1-4525-9029-5 (sc)
ISBN: 978-1-4525-9031-8 (hc)
ISBN: 978-1-4525-9030-1 (e)

Library of Congress Control Number: 2014900628

Balboa Press rev. date: 3/10/2016

To my boys.
To Mykel, for your sensitive and loving heart. You have
taught me so much about allowing others to find their
own paths. I learned many life lessons along our journey
together. I am so proud of the man you have become.
To Jesse Alexander, for your wisdom and courage.
You have helped me clarify my own soul's path.
I am amazed at your ability to help others and
remain steadfast in your true purpose.

CONTENTS

PREFACE

I have been a counselor for more than twenty-five years and have worked with children that had special needs and children who have suffered abuse. Not only did I deal with sensory processing/regulation problems on a professional level, but I also did on a personal level—my husband and I have children with these same issues. They had learning issues and multiple diagnoses as they were growing up. I worked and lived the concept of sensory processing. Some people would say that I was lucky to work in the field and have children like this at home. I initially disagreed, but I came to understand that this was part of my life purpose.

I began teaching about sensory processing to other parents and professionals when my children were young. People would ask me if I had a website or a book. This inspired me to write our family story. I began perceiving what others considered medical or therapeutic "problems" as assets. Children may process information differently, but in our family, we see the benefits in this, not the challenges. I am sharing our life experiences, trials, and triumphs.

This book is written with my understanding of sensory processing, what my children were like when they were young, and their perceptions of how they are as adults. We hope that this provides some guidance for other families going through the same experience.

Acknowledgments

I want to thank both of my boys, Mykel and Jesse, along with my friend Kathy Robinson, for their memories and help with the book. This was truly a labor of love. At times I even felt the birthing pains! Thanks to my husband, David, for his patience with our process. I want to thank my incredible group of friends who offered help by reading my work and offering their honest opinions. I want to thank my dear friends Patsy Kuhn, Jamie Britton, and Linda Harrelson for helping my distracted writings become a clear book.

Finally, I want to thank God for his help and guidance in writing this book. Although my knowledge of *Sensory Integration* has been with me for years, my husband and I were shown much more of the way our bodies work and the purpose of these special children. Initially, I planned to focus only on sensory processing, but we were shown so much more in the spiritual connection that the book evolved.

CHAPTER 1

OUR STORY

"You're pregnant" are words parents long to hear. Even with a great pregnancy, parents can be overwhelmed with caring for their children. This is more apparent when a child has behaviors that families do not understand. If the family faces issues with the pregnancy, birth trauma, or the dreaded fact that something is not right with the child, then "How can I care for this child?" races through their minds. We naturally parent children the way we were taught, either by our own parents or maybe through a few classes attended. Rarely are parents given the skills to handle children who do not fit the "normal" way of developing. My husband and I faced this in our own journey with our boys. We want to share the lessons we learned along the way in order to help others. We learned about sensory integration as a way to help our boys calm their bodies. This helped us not to label the things the boys did as behavioral problems but how their bodies worked for regulation. The most important lesson for us was the way our family grew in spiritual connection. We hope our stories help others along their journeys.

Sensory integration, or processing, is simply how we use information through our senses to connect with what we have already learned about the world around us. We take in information through our five senses: taste, vision, hearing, touch, and smell, along with two hidden senses. We use movement through our vestibular sense (in the inner ear) and our proprioceptive sense (in our muscles and joints) to help us move about and calm our bodies. The sensory system was not understood well when I was born in the 1960s. Today, most of the general population has not heard of these concepts, only those who have or know children who are struggling to learn to regulate their bodies.

When I was a young child, my mother told stories about driving me around town so that I would sleep. She would say that as soon as she pulled in the driveway I would wake up. She stated that I did not sleep for the first three years of my life. She said I would sit and eat lemons while watching the Johnny Cash show. Not understanding the sensory issues that I had as a child, my mother would state, "We just beat the hell out of you." When I married my husband, David, I could easily identify with some of his behaviors. He has a hard time with meeting new people and large crowds, and he prefers routines. So when I talk about sensory integration/processing to others, I often say that David and I should have never bred. Two adults with similar problems were running the risk of having children with these issues. As young adults, we were eager to have children of our own. We suffered through four miscarriages, and finally two beautiful boys came into our lives.

Mykel David

Our first son, Mykel, was conceived right after a miscarriage and before my husband left for the first Gulf War. I had already scheduled to see a specialist, Dr. Brown, to help us get pregnant. Due to complications, I could not get in right away to see Dr. Brown. When I finally was able to see the specialist, I was five months along. I believe this was God's way of helping me pass the three-month mark where I had lost children before. At this time, I did not fully understand how emotional stress was affecting my unborn child. My family was in turmoil over losing my three-year-old nephew after eighteen months of cancer treatments. My sister-in-law was losing her precious child just as I finally had one.

The day I drove my husband to the air force base with war looming, my anxiety was very high. He was leaving on a mission, and he was not allowed to know where he was going until the plane was in the air. With the escalation in the Gulf, I was stressed and worried as to where he was going to be stationed. I drove home worrying about my unborn son and my husband. I turned on the television to see the starting of the first Gulf War. I do not typically show a lot of emotions, but at that moment, I collapsed on the floor, crying. My thoughts raced. *What will happen to David? What will happen if I have to raise my son alone? What about all those serving? We have friends who are already in Iraq. What will happen to them?* I cried out in prayer for all those in the service.

We had not been at war in so long, and the treatment of the Vietnam veterans ran through the back of my mind. Of course, all this changed, and the country did show tremendous support. Now, looking back, I can only imagine the amount of stress hormones that were being dumped into my body as I carried Mykel. Luckily, my husband was able to return home before Mykel's birth.

Mykel was two weeks overdue. After some complications, it was decided that he would be delivered by Caesarean section. Dr. Brown had an incredible sense of humor. During the delivery, Dr. Brown exclaimed, "This is not a baby—this is a football player. This is not an umbilical cord—this is a rope." Mykel was eleven pounds and six ounces. He was twenty-three and three-quarter inches long and bow-legged! Our little baby boy we had tried so hard to get here was huge! A few hours after he delivered Mykel, Dr. Brown came into the room and stated that Mykel had a romantic date. "He will have to go to the nursery tonight, because I just delivered a redheaded ten-pound, eight-ounce baby girl."

I noticed right away that Mykel and I had difficulty bonding. He did not like to be held. He did not tolerate certain clothing and was susceptible to rashes. He would not sleep at night. He cried often and there was little that would comfort him. He had projectile vomiting, allergies to milk, asthma, and extreme allergies to everything outside. To say that Mykel was an active child would be an understatement. He never slowed down; he walked by the age of nine months. He talked early, was very bright, and charmed all those around him.

Being a counselor, I knew the importance of bonding and self-regulation. I had been trained in *attachment theory*. Attachment is crucial to children learning how to form relationships. Mykel had extreme crying outbursts, especially around sleep. I read many books and tried so many methods. I tried the Faber method of getting Mykel to sleep. (Allow the child to stay in the room, check on child, offer reassurance, but do not pick the child up or take him to your bed.) I worked months trying to get him to sleep in his room and through the night. At this time, I was working with the early intervention program, especially with children who had autism. I began working with several occupational therapists, who taught me *sensory integration* techniques. I began asking questions about my son as well. One therapist, named Keri, told me, "Quit torturing the child." She showed me how to make his crib feel smaller (by sectioning it off into smaller areas with rolled towels). This induced a more secure feeling for Mykel. We used heavy blankets for deep pressure into his muscles and joints. We played soothing music to limit other sounds. He began sleeping better, although even to this day he struggles with sleep.

Even when he was very young, we knew Mykel had regulatory issues. He was very obsessive-compulsive and hyperactive. He would either over-attend to tasks, such as working puzzles upside down on the non-printed side for hours, or not focus on important details, letters, numbers, and reading. He had signs of dyslexia, writing everything as a mirror image. Mostly he would have emotional outbursts that would last twenty to forty minutes. He would not tolerate help with calming down. Since I was a therapist, I tried very hard to follow the ADHD (Attention Deficit Hyperactivity Disorder) treatments that did not use medication.

After Mykel had attended pre-K and kindergarten and was beginning T1 (transition first grade) without learning his letters or numbers, we knew we were going to need help. His emotional outbursts had taken a toll on our family and his caregivers. We started ADHD medication—and within one month, he began to read. He also tolerated his younger brother without emotional outbursts. At the time, it felt like a miracle to us.

I know that so many parents struggle with the guilt of medicating their children or using more natural methods. We have used both, and my view on these has changed over the years. This can be a confusing and frustrating process. Although I encourage parents to get professional help and have their child evaluated, including a thorough medical exam, I advise them that *they* are the parents and they know their child better than anyone else. I tell them to trust their instincts and do what fits for their family.

My boys did use medication when they were younger, and we used more natural methods when they were teenagers. Now they are adults, and they try to manage without either. It is still a struggle. Parents can be weighed down by guilt over the choices they have made. They must realize that there are benefits to all choices. Most parents are doing the very best they can at that moment in time. Most parents' choices are made through loving intentions. It is their support and love that is the key. It is the parents' connection with the children that makes the difference.

Jesse Alexander

Almost three years after Mykel's birth, we went through our fourth miscarriage; this was in January 1994. My new obstetrician stated that we needed to wait three months before getting pregnant again. My husband told her that was not a problem, since he was being deployed for three months and that we were done trying to have children. In March 1994, I became pregnant during the few days that David was home. My doctor was surprised; she remarked, "You guys barely waited."

Right away we had difficulty hearing the baby's heartbeat. We had fourteen ultrasounds due to the issues of this pregnancy. (Because my husband was being deployed, he was only present for two of the ultrasounds) At three months, I hemorrhaged and was rushed to the hospital to have a D&C, since they could not see a fetus in the blood. (I was bleeding so much that I scared an OB nurse practitioner of more than twenty years.)

At the last minute, my doctor decided to do an ultrasound. I could not look at the ultrasound screen. I stared at the ceiling, knowing that David would not try again. I was resigned to the fact that I would only have my little boy, Mykel. At this moment, my husband jumped up and screamed, "He's in there, and he's kicking. He is mad as hell!" The bleeding stopped, and I was put on bed rest for one month. At the five-month mark, I began leaking amniotic fluid, but I only knew that it felt like I was having wetting accidents (enuresis). One of the ultrasounds showed that the amniotic fluid was gone, although the technician never said a word; looking back, I knew something was wrong. My doctor called me at nine in the evening (which is never a good sign). She told me that the amniotic fluid was gone. She said she was very sorry, but I needed to come in the next morning and make some decisions. She kept telling me apologetically that the baby would not be viable at five months if we had to deliver it. She asked that I bring someone with me.

David and my friend Kathy Robinson accompanied me to the visit. My doctor explained that at five months, babies begin to make the amniotic fluid, rather than the mother. Something could be wrong with the baby if it was not making enough fluid. Or I could have had a rupture and lost the fluid. I explained that I had been leaking fluid. She declared, "In that case, it is much like an abscessed tooth." She explained that, due to the rupture, an infection could develop, which could endanger my life. At this point, the baby would not survive, being only five months' gestation. She requested that we make a decision about abortion. I could not abort this child. I knew in my soul that he needed to be here and that I could not take his life. She stated, "You are allowing nature to take its course."

Although I readily said yes, I noticed David was very agitated. The doctor discussed the issues of the child being born without amniotic fluid during pregnancy. The child could have issues with his internal organs not developing, or he could have brain damage. The lungs might not form correctly, or there could be developmental delays, and we might still have to take the baby before it was ready. I was told to go back on bed rest for another month and take my temperature daily to monitor for infection. The doctor informed us that the chance of the rupture healing itself was minimal. Afterward, my husband stated that he was not sure he could handle a child with special needs. I was working in the field of early intervention and knew I could handle whatever was to come, but I was not sure if I would do this alone.

Jesse was born in December, at three weeks' earlier gestation than his brother. The doctor wanted to make sure we would only have an eight-pound baby. Jesse's birth was a planned C-section. When he was born, he weighed eleven pounds eleven ounces and had a chest that measured fifteen and half inches. Everyone in the delivery room was shocked! He was a healthy baby boy without medical problems. Everyone kept saying, "Do you know what a miracle he is?" My doctor came into my room and, with tears in her eyes, discussed what a miracle this was. I knew how special my children were, because I knew how hard it had been to get them here.

Having difficulty getting through the birth process is an indicator that there could be sensory problems. We do know that birth trauma and prematurity cause issues with sensory development. In hindsight, I see that my boys had sensory issues in the making.

Children with Sensory Issues

We have stated that Mykel was "active"—we did not know that you could double that activity in a child named Jesse. Jesse's list of so-called problems included frantic feeding, tremors (especially upon waking from sleep), difficulty nursing, and constant ear infections, starting at one month of age. By the time he was two, doctors had discovered that he had no openings in the sinus cavities. He had surgery to open the sinus cavities and remove "glue ear" substance (which can cause hearing issues) from the ear canal, and he had his adenoids removed. He was then in the early intervention program, due to delays in speech, social skills, and self-help skills.

Jesse had poor motor planning (the way in which the brain organizes motor movements). He received both occupational therapy and speech therapy. He did not speak until three and a half years of age. At that age, he only spoke with vowels and no consonants. His articulation was not clear to most people until age eight. He stuttered, had tremors, and was extremely active. His attention at age three was two seconds per object.

When Jesse was four, we had moved to Biloxi, Mississippi. We met our new pediatrician, Dr. Couch. Our first visit was to take Mykel in for a refill check on his ADHD medication. During this visit, Jesse was either hanging from the coat rack on the wall or climbing the chairs. When I asked the doctor for help on testing Jesse, there was not a question in her mind. She said in the meantime to give him some of his brother's medication to see whether that would work. She did not want to wait for his appointment, as it was an apparent, immediate need. I thought, *At least someone else is seeing what I deal with each day.*

God had placed us in a special area. We were blocks from Biloxi Regional Medical Center. Shortly after we moved there, Jesse began having multiple issues. Dr. Couch worked closely with all the specialists at this hospital. We saw a pediatric developmental specialist, the pediatric neurologist, and the pediatric cardiologist, as well as many more physicians. These wonderful professionals helped us walk through this challenging time. Jesse already had the diagnosis of developmental delays and ADHD. He began either turning white, lethargic, and passing out (heart rate as low as thirty) or becoming red faced, out of breath, and exhausted (heart rate as high as two hundred). He was diagnosed with POTS (postural orthostatic tachycardia syndrome) and at age nine was diagnosed with Tourette's. Our pediatric cardiologist, Dr. Boris, was the first to diagnose Jesse with POTS. We were trying different medications to help stop his passing out and to regulate his heart rate.

At one point, Jesse was hospitalized to begin a certain medication. I was saying again how my active little boy now seemed to just lie on the couch all the time. Dr. Boris told me, "You have to get over this. He is not the same child now and never will be." I was shocked into reality. I was still holding on to the way it had been and not seeing Jesse for who he was now. I was grieving the loss of the child that I'd had. I was grieving the loss of my hope for a healthy child. I was grieving the loss of our life and the plans we had made for our bright, active young boy. This wonderful doctor referred us on to Dr. Blair Grubb.

We eventually saw the specialist, Dr. Grubb, in Toledo, Ohio. He is an amazing physician. On our first visit to him, we flew into Toledo from Oklahoma. We waited hours in the waiting room (with my hyperactive child). While we were in the waiting room, people were comparing how far they had driven and saying that Dr. Grubb was worth the wait. Finally, at 5:30 p.m., we were able to get in.

Dr. Grubb listened to Jesse's symptoms. He got up, brought back his laptop, and went through a PowerPoint presentation that he used to teach other students and doctors. I was amazed that what he was talking about was my son. He explained that the condition was caused by a bad spot on Jesse's brain stem.

It sent out a faulty signal through his autonomic nervous system. Although none of this could be corrected, he gave us skills to live a more normal life. He then questioned whether Jesse had autism (at that time, Jesse did not make good eye contact and had lots of sensory symptoms). We discussed his developmental issues.

Then the doctor said, "We need to discuss you." He stated, "I know counselors, and they tend to take care of everyone else and not themselves." He told me, "When you have a chronically ill child …" Those words hit me like a ton of bricks. "Chronically ill" was a weight, and at the same time it was liberating to know that our struggle was acknowledged. Dr. Grubb then talked about things I could do with Jesse the next day, such as the Toledo Zoo and restaurants he would tolerate well. When we walked out of his office, it was 7:30 p.m., dark outside, and we were the only ones left around.

The next day, Jesse and I had a lovely day at the zoo and then flew home. Two days after I had seen Dr. Grubb, in my mailbox there was a book from him, called *When Bad Things Happen to Good People*. I broke down in tears. We finally had confirmation of our challenges, but more importantly, we had it from such a caring soul. Dr. Grubb is an amazing doctor, not just because of his knowledge and compassion but because he is a *master* at being present in the moment. When you are with him, the outside chaos does not matter. He is there for you and your needs. He is humble, caring, and loving. There is no feeling of being rushed; you feel you are being heard. We saw him a few more times—even as Dr. Grubb battled his own fight with cancer. It was an honor to have had our time with him. We are eternally grateful to this physician and to his wonderful staff.

Jesse and I were flying back from Toledo one year later, when David's aunt went into hospice. My husband picked us up from the airport, and we started driving to Tennessee. When Jesse would get sick or tired, his symptoms would escalate. On the road trip, Jesse began clearing his throat incessantly. His dad kept asking if he needed a drink. Then it hit me. I knew what this was—Tourette's symptoms. By the time we returned home, Jesse was flailing his arms back every time he attempted a task. If he was doing homework, Jesse could barely write a few letters before a tremor would hit and he would flail his arms backward along with his upper body and head. This caused him to lose his place in his work. This happened over and over.

As a parent, it is painful to watch your child try so hard and his body not cooperate. Most people hear the word Tourette's and think of those that cuss spontaneously but that occurs on the rare end of the spectrum. Most individuals have eye twitches, motor tics, flailing, or jerking limbs.

After Jesse's diagnosis, we returned to Toledo. I updated Dr. Grubb on Jesse's changes. He suggested that Jesse should go into the theater. He explained that when people with Tourette's or those that stutter are on the stage, they operate out of a different part of their brains. So on the stage, individuals do not have those symptoms. At this moment, I looked over at my very shy little boy and thought, *Theater?* Years later, Jesse entered college as a theater major, with becoming a director as his goal. Jesse has a commanding presence on stage—without any Tourette's symptoms.

We followed the medical recommendations (increased salt intake, medications, methods to respond to Jesse's passing out, etc.), but we started limiting the number of doctor's appointments. It was to the point that life was revolving around the medical world, and we had lost our time together. We started only going to the specialist once a year, since there were no treatments to solve the issue. Unless something new came up, we did not go to the doctor. It was amazing that the quality of life changed for us. Jesse was able to be more normalized in his play and everyday tasks.

Both of our children taught us so many life lessons. We had opportunity to use sensory integration techniques on a daily basis. It was up and down, with great trials on some days and great successes on others.

As we work through each of the sensory areas, I will share what worked for our family, and I will report how the boys see their lives today. What we did not expect to learn was how these unique children use their gifts to connect spiritually and to help others. This is a life lesson. So many children struggle with sensory integration but display spiritual gifts as well. My hope in writing this book is that our life story will help other families along their journeys.

When I started this book, I promised myself to be completely honest and straightforward, including all of our struggles and failures as well as our triumphs. My initial purpose was to write specifically about sensory integration, what it is, and how it affected our lives. As a counselor, I am trained in scientific approaches: you state your hypothesis (belief) and go about proving it with unbiased research. Initially it was very difficult for me to believe that I needed to add the spiritual side to this book. I thought that I would write that part as the next book. You know the old saying, "If you want to make God laugh, make plans." God, Higher Power, Spirit—whatever you may choose to call the One that is everything—had different ideas. I know this will be hard for some people to believe or understand. All I know is that I must tell our story completely.

Jesse was born with unique gifts. He has always had the gift of wisdom beyond his years. He has been able to see things that I cannot see or prove the existence of. When he finally was able to communicate with words, around four years of age, Jesse was always talking about the "shadow people." When we moved to Biloxi, Mississippi, Jesse would often walk down the hallway and say, "Mom, Jesus says …" and then, looking back over his shoulder, he would turn back and say, "Nope, he says he is just an angel."

I would respond with "I'll take an angel." Another example of Jesse's knowledge included information about events. Coming from Oklahoma, Mykel was frightened by tornado warnings. Right after we moved to Biloxi, we were living on Keesler Air Force Base. We had heard a tornado warning, and Mykel yelled, "No, not here too!" There was a tornado dropping down out of the clouds over Keesler. We were all in the bathroom, and Mykel was extremely upset. My mom and I began praying. The house was very dark, and the storm had that loud roar that you get with a tornado.

Jesse said, so calmly, "Budders (brother), it's okay. Jesus gonna bust the storm up." It turned quiet, and a light came in under the bathroom door. I walked out to the back door, and there was a hole in the clouds right above our home, and the clouds looked as if they were "busting up."

So, as I struggled with whether or not to mention these special gifts in this book, I knew in my heart that so many other parents face these moments without an explanation as to why their children do certain things. Maybe they are struggling to believe in their child. They may want to say to the child, "It's just your imagination." They may have family members discounting their experiences.

Our family faced those things and so many more. I know that every time Jesse interacts with others, even if at first they don't believe the message he is giving them, they often come back a short time later and say, "You know what Jesse said? Well, that was true."

I know that I am not the only parent dealing with children like Jesse. In fact, Doreen Virtue has written often about what she calls the *rainbow, indigo,* and *crystal children.* I believe that my purpose in life is that of what she calls a light worker. I have always known that I shine God's light. Even when I was a young child, strangers would come up to me and tell me their life stories. When I was eight years old, my mom and I were in a grocery checkout line, when a woman in her thirties told me all about her divorce. As we walked out, my mom said, "I don't know why people tell you stuff like that!"

I believe that Mykel was born as an indigo child. Doreen Virtue describes indigo children as passionate, loving but here to take on the injustice of the world and struggle with righteous anger. Mykel has passion about things he believes are important. He also has anger at the injustice in the world. Mykel can sense things around him. He knows when people are not being straightforward. He has always been very sensitive to the energy of others. When people are fighting, they may have left the room, but then Mykel could walk into that room and begin to cry or get upset. This sensitivity has led him into behaviors of withdrawal, anger, and short-term drug use.

Jesse has many of signs of a crystal child. Doreen Virtue describes crystal children as also having the ability to see through other's fake façades. Crystal children are also very loving in nature and have many spiritual gifts. Jesse is my gentle giant. He is loving, but he can see straight through the fake front some people put on. He sees right through to the hearts of others. If you are not open and honest, then he has little patience or time for you. He does not tolerate those who are wrapped in their egos and focused on the trappings of this world. Crystal children are very different to raise.

Doreen Virtue has written many beautiful books describing these children, and if you believe you have a child like this, please educate yourself on their ways and purposes in life. I will be writing about our path in raising these boys. When we were raising our children, resources like Doreen Virtue's books were not available. I will share what worked and what didn't at times—again, so that you may learn something from our story. These special children, indigo, crystal, and rainbow children being born in more numbers since the 1970s.

While raising our boys, we found very little information on how to work with our children. The old ways of thinking and punishment—"suck it up and don't cry" or "pull yourself up by your boot straps"—have little effect on these children. The way they process and learn is different. The way you interact with them is different. These children require your "A" game every day. They will hold you accountable for the choices you make, because their purpose is great. They need your very best so they can move forward. This is important, because they are the children who will show us the way to a greater connection to God. I hope that in some way we can offer hope for you on your journey.

Chapter 2

Sensory Integration

Medical Definition

Sensory integration dysfunction was first theorized by Jean Ayres, PhD, OTR (occupational therapist). She stated that sensory integration was the ability to organize information from our senses to be used by the brain. Someone with *sensory integration dysfunction* (SID) would have a decreased ability to organize the information that comes through the senses. The information would be sensed, but it would be registered, interpreted, or processed differently by the brain (Ayres, 1979). *Sensory processing disorder* (SPD) is a neurological disorder causing issues in the taking in, processing, and responding to information relayed by the senses about the environment. These include gustatory (oral), visual, auditory, tactile (touch), olfactory (smell), proprioception (muscle and joints), and vestibular (balance/inner ear). Although in the current medical literature SPD and SID are interchangeable, many committed individuals are working diligently on research and clarification of these diagnoses. Currently SPD is not recognized in standard medical manuals, including DSM-IV-TR, DSM-5, (Diagnostic Statistical Manual of Mental Health which psychologists use for diagnosis) or ICD-10

(International Classification of Diseases which physicians use for diagnosis). SPD is mentioned in Stanley Greenspan's *Diagnostic Manual for Infancy and Early Childhood* and under Regulation Disorders of Sensory Processing in the Zero to Three diagnostic classification.

Lucy J Miller, PhD, OTR, and many others who are doing research, have defined the disorder as sensory processing disorder (SPD). They have divided it into three sub-areas:

Sensory Modulation Disorder (SMD): (I was taught this included attention, regulation, and modulation.) Sensory over responsiveness, sensory under responsiveness, sensory craving, which includes fearful, negative-seeking, and stubborn or self-absorbed behaviors.

Sensory Based Motor Disorder (SBMD): (I was taught this involved the two hidden senses and motor planning.) Dyspraxia and postural disorder, which shows motor output that is disorganized.

Sensory Discrimination Disorder (SDD): (I was taught this was sensory defensiveness.) Incorrect processing of information, including visual, touch, auditory, taste, position, and interoception (Miller, 2007).

The Sensory Processing Disorder Foundation, the STAR (Sensory Therapies and Research) Center in Denver, and others, are working hard to provide research and treatment options.

Important points

- It was first developed by Jean Ayres, PhD, OTR, in her book *Sensory Integration and the Child*.
- The sensory integration system allows the information from our senses to be put together with prior information, memories, and knowledge stored in the brain in order for us to make meaningful response.
- Sensory integration occurs in the central nervous system and is generally thought to take place in the spinal column, midbrain, and brain-stem levels.
- It is responsible for coordination, attention, arousal levels, autonomic functioning, emotions, memory, and higher-level cognitive functions.
- Sensory processing is the brain activity that locates, identifies, and gives meaning to sensation.
- We all use our five senses and the two hidden senses.
- The five apparent senses and the two hidden senses— vestibular (inner ear-balance) and proprioceptive (muscle and joint movement)—take information to the brain to be processed together with what the brain has already learned.

Layman's Terms

Sensory integration or sensory processing is the way our senses take in information and our brain combines this information with what it already knows and understands. We all learn in kindergarten about the five senses (taste, vision, hearing, touch, smell), but what we do not understand is the hidden senses, the proprioceptive (muscle and joints) and vestibular (movement) ones. We will also look at the internal sense of energy (tiredness or alertness) called *interoception*, and external sensing energy called *exteroception*.

During the birth process, as a baby travels through the birth canal, it gets lots of proprioceptive input to help the brain and body organize. (Some research shows that a high percentage of children with sensory issues are born by C-sections.) Babies are then rocked and held, which gives them more vestibular and proprioceptive-sensory input. At this time, we offer a baby the bottle or nursing and work on the oral-motor muscles and the suck-swallow-breathe sequencing. Developing these systems is important for everyone to learn self-regulation. We use these systems from the time we are born until we die. As toddlers, we spend hours climbing up and down, rolling around, swinging, and mouthing objects. As children, we spend most of our time in physical play, learning sports, and being active. We continue to use this regulation as adults by taking a walk when we get stressed. Many people smoke, drink, overeat, or chew on pens, etc. to regulate. In essence, we use movement—our muscles and joints, and our mouths—to regulate our bodies. Most of the time this is done with little knowledge of what is occurring in our bodies. When the sensory system does not work well together, we have some of the following issues.

■ Attention, Modulation, and Regulation: Sensory Modulation Disorder (SMD)

Attention reflects the brain's own activity level. This affects concentration, physical activity, emotional levels, and modulation. Modulation is the flow of sensory information coming into the central nervous system (CNS). Modulation issues can be compared to the 0–60 mph, going from slow to fast with little in between, rather than living in the middle. This modulation is also used in expressing emotions. Children who have too little or too much emotional expression are said to have modulation issues.

Attention requires the ability to screen out nonessential sensory information and background noises, such as lights flickering, other people talking, and appliance or fan noises. I was taught that regulation issues were connected to sensory processing, arousal levels, modulation (especially of emotions) and the way in which we communicate needs.

■ Sensory Defensiveness: Oral, Tactile, Auditory, Olfactory, Visual, Movement: Sensory Discrimination Disorder (SDD)

I love explaining sensory defensiveness in a group, because either people start pointing fingers at each other or they say, "I know someone like that." I begin by explaining the stress cycle, because all adults understand the stress cycle. We talk about the stress chemicals and how difficult it is to calm down once you are stressed. Then I talk about how people with sensory defensiveness have the stress cycle turned on by everyday input, like touch. Sensory defensiveness can occur to anyone at any time. Individuals can become sensory defensive if they go through traumatic events, medical treatment such as cancer therapies, and of course, difficult-birth trauma. Children born prematurely or with significant birth trauma are taken into neonatal intensive care (NICU) units that have bright lights, loud sounds, and painful stimuli. Typically, NICUs limit holding of the child. Comparing this to rocking, swaddling, and feeding of a typical newborn will demonstrate how the brain can be wired differently. The babies with prematurity or birth trauma have the stress cycle turned on, with typical sensory input. The brain perceives typical touch as too much and responds with an alerting response. This causes the baby to not tolerate touch or being held, or to not calm with movement. These babies grow up with issues of clothing bothering them, especially tags, textures, seams on socks, or tightly tied shoes. Children may have issues with eating different textures or mixing textures of food (for example, stew or soups). They may then have limited food choices due to their intolerance of textures. Children may under or overreact to sounds, visual stimuli, or smells. Children may become very rigid in how they deal with the world due to the stress cycle continually begin turned on with normal input.

Important points

- Fight, flight, and fright reactions are stress responses to sensory input.
- Hyper responsiveness to touch or other sensory input creates sensory defensiveness.
- Fears related to sounds or noises can be complicated by sensory defensiveness.
- Hypersensitivity to light and avoidance of eye contact are signs of visual overstimulation.
- Oral defensiveness (intolerance) to textures or temperature can cause issues with eating for example a picky eater.

Vestibular /Proprioceptive (Movement): Sensory-Based Motor Disorder (SBMD), Dyspraxia, Postural Disorder

When these systems do not work well, multiple issues may arise. These systems regulate muscle tone, motor planning, and the protective system. Muscle tone refers to the strength in the muscles. You can see this in children who are stiff (high muscle tone) or those we call "floppy" (low muscle tone).

Protective System

The protective system shields us from dangers. This is the system that helped the cave man run from a predator. When the stress cycle is kicked on, chemicals are produced that motivate the body to move away from danger. Unfortunately, in today's society we do not use movement as a way to deal with stress. Our bodies are subject to chronic stress, and the stress-cycle chemicals, such as cortisol, are stored in our bodies. The chronic stress of today has been linked to heart disease, cancers, etc. There is a great book called *Why Zebras Don't Get Ulcers*, by Robert M. Sapolsky. He did research on those who handle stress well. He found four psychological variables in those that did well with stress. People who were successful had a sense of *control* in their lives, they had predictable *routines*, healthy *outlets* for frustrations, and they had a good sense of *threat perception*. These people could screen out the things not to stress about and were able to pay attention to real threats of danger (Sapolsky, 2005).

With the children I have worked with over the years, I have seen that these issues were ones that they could not handle. Foster children lose that sense of control as soon as they are removed from home. They have learned poor regulation, so their outlets for frustration are usually screaming, hitting, fighting, etc. Many have never had predictable routines before they came to a foster home. These children typically have hyper vigilance (being on guard) as a survival mechanism. This causes their threat perception to be high for any event. They tend to think most things are a threat.

Children with protective systems that are not processing information correctly will have an overstimulated system and become hypersensitive, or they will have an under stimulated system, with hyposensitivity.

Mykel had an overstimulated system but with a slight delay in processing. He would become overly upset about small things. He also did not process danger well. Children like this will run into the street without looking, climb too high without knowing how to get down, or get into things without thinking. Mykel always seemed to be getting into everything. Even when his father and I were near Mykel, he impulsively got into a cactus, battery acid, and gasoline, which he drank. Sitting in the backseat of his aunt's car, Mykel once stuck a car cigarette lighter onto his thumb. He held it there until his aunt smelled the burning flesh. When she yelled, "What are you doing?" Mykel let it go, looked at it, and then screamed.

Jesse was on the hyposensitive side. Jesse did not perceive pain. If Jesse complained about hurting, it was usually too late. He would wake up and complain about his ear and that day we would see the doctor. The doctor would be shocked that his eardrum would be at the point of bursting. In fact, Jesse would never respond to doctors looking at his reflexes. I watched two neurologists work fifteen minutes trying to get a response to any stimulus. Jesse would lose teeth and not know it. He would come in to brush his teeth, and I would notice a missing tooth and ask him where it was. He would say, "I don't know." He would have the same response for bruises I noticed after school. The danger with these children who do not perceive pain is that they can injure themselves seriously and not get help.

There are also issues with poor tactile discrimination. This is when the touch system picks up on input and is not sure what it is. The brain does not process what the input is. The brain basically says, "Huh?"

Main Points on the Stress Cycle

- Stress is the physiological process of arousal to prepare the individual to meet a perceived challenge/stress event.
- Energy is stored in the muscles and tissues for activity.
- Heart and lung functions increase for use of oxygen and glucose.
- Anabolism (digestion, growth, immunity, etc.) is suppressed until emergency is survived.
- Inflammatory responses are suppressed during stress.
- Pain perception is blunted.
- The sympathetic nervous system is activated: epinephrine and norepinephrine are released; the pancreas secretes glucagon; there is adrenal release of glucocorticoids; the pituitary goes to work releasing B-endorphin, prolactin, and vasopressin (as mentioned, the parasympathetic nervous system which includes sex and growth hormones, is suppressed).
- Symptoms include irritability, restlessness, fatigue, difficulty concentrating, difficulty sleeping or restless sleep, worry, fear, rumination, and apprehension.

- Cognition initially becomes sharp, but then it narrows its focus, and later there is long-term stress marked by difficulty in concentration, confusion, and indecision.
- Behaviors to expect include—what humans do best under stress—to freeze, flee, fight, withdraw, pursue, or use anxiety-binding mechanisms (gossip, eating, drinking, exercise, prayer, meditation, etc.)
- Four psychological variables—what humans can do well to help with stress—include improving sense of control, ensuring predictable routines, providing good outlets for frustrations, and screening out threats well.

Autonomic Nervous System

The autonomic nervous system is located in the spinal cord, brain stem, and internal organs and comprised of three parts: the sympathetic, parasympathetic, and the enteric. The system mobilizes the body for the fight-or-flight response. The sympathetic and parasympathetic are systems of balance. Their purpose is to maintain homeostasis.

The sympathetic nervous system aids in the control of the body's internal organs and response of the fight-or-flight reaction.

The parasympathetic system generally works on the body at a state of rest and digestion.

The enteric nervous system governs the gastrointestinal system. It is a complex system of neurons, neurotransmitters, and special proteins responsible for communications. It is sometimes called the second brain due to the communication that is like "thinking," "remembering," and "learning." This is a fascinating system from which you can learn how what you eat affects how you think.

The functions include coordination of reflexes, and it can operate independently of the brain and spinal cord. It communicates to the parasympathetic nervous systems through the vagus nerve, but even if the nerve is severed or damaged, the system would continue to function. The vagus nerve is amazing! It is the tenth of the twelve cranial nerves. This nerve communicates sensory information about the state of the body's organs to the central nervous system. If you have ever seen this in a human body map, it will make sense to you how the hearing, equilibrium, taste, breathing (suck-swallow-breath sequence) and the stomach (nausea) are so closely tied together—because they are tied through this nerve. This nerve basically tells the brain what the body is doing and transmits outgoing information.

What does all of this mean? Well, for Jesse's sake, as parents we needed to educate ourselves and was critical that we learn his symptoms and treatment. Dr. Blair Grubb wrote a book called *Syncope: Mechanisms and Management*. Basically, he explained the process of this system and explained why some people have episodes of passing out (or syncope). Jesse's bad spot on his brain was the reason his autonomic nervous system did not work well. Even when other doctors discussed a pacemaker for Jesse, Dr. Grubb was able to explain that this would not change the response his body was having, since it was coming from the brain stem. Jesse had poor temperature control, heart-rate issues, breathing trouble, intestinal issues, etc. So even if a pacemaker were regulating his heart rate, his body would still react with the autonomic response.

One of the most extreme examples of his nervous system's behavior occurred after we moved to an Air Force base in Oklahoma. We were painting and working on a rental house. We had moved to Biloxi when Jesse was four years old, and now he was eight years old, but he did not remember snow. This particular day, it had snowed several inches. Jesse learned to make a snowball, and he and his brother made an igloo. They played outside for several hours. That evening Jesse complained to his brother that his chest hurt. (This was not a typical symptom when he had a syncope episode). Mykel brought him to me. Jesse was looking pale, so I had him lie down. I started checking his pulse, which was dropping drastically from 125, to 90, and then to 70, so I called 911. They responded right away; our local fire station had a firefighter who also had an eight-year-old with heart problems. We were soon surrounded by five firefighters, with more outside.

Jesse's oxygen saturation was low. They put oxygen on him, and he began coughing. When the ambulance arrived, the attendant asked how long Jesse had been coughing, and I told him it had started when the oxygen was put on him. They took Jesse out to the ambulance, and at this time he turned red in the face, his temperature spiked to 105, and heart rate was 185 to 190. We rushed to Children's Hospital, where Jesse would pass out. When he came to, he screamed, "Owie, owie!" but passed out before telling us where he was hurting. After a chest x-ray, Jesse was diagnosed with pneumonia, partially collapsed lung, and pleurisy.

We knew when he got sick that it would be a difficult issue, but this was such an extreme response and we had had so little warning. In this episode, the delicate balance between the sympathetic and parasympathetic systems was evident.

When you live with someone whose body not only doesn't cooperate but actually threatens the life at times, it takes a toll on you emotionally. I saw it in the firefighter's eyes that night, even though it was not his son. It's the same look I saw in my stepbrother's eyes after he lost his three-year-old to cancer. I have seen it in the eyes of hundreds of parents when they are finding out the diagnosis to some developmental problem their child has. It is hurt, pain, and grief, but mainly it is the shame and guilt we feel that we cannot fix this. As parents we want to fix our children's problems—at least that has been taught to us—but in reality, we are just the souls who are there to help them through the journey, not take it away from them. We are there to help but not fix it for them. This knowledge will not take away the look in parents' eyes, but it can give them a purpose in the journey.

Level of Arousal

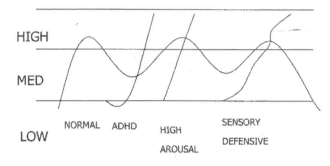

Level of arousal is important when we look at day-to-day functioning and see how medication affects behavioral issues. On typical days, everyone goes through up and downs with their level of arousal. They may wake up and need a coffee or Coke to get started. They may do fine until after lunch and then get tired and sleepy. They may have a burst of energy after work and then crash at night.

Children with ADHD are low-arousal children. They are often hard to get up. When they do get up, they have a hard time with modulation (remember the 0-60 mph sprint); they bounce right into the high-arousal range. This is why stimulant medication works for them. The medicine brings them into the middle range, and they do not have to bounce so high. Mykel was a low-arousal child. He was very hard to get up. For years, it was a struggle to get him out the door. He would have daily crying episodes. He would scream, "You don't love me," when I was trying to get him dressed and off to school. Really, his truth was, "I can't function yet in the morning and need to wake up on my own." To this day he struggles with early mornings. He has multiple alarm clocks and sleeps sometimes on the couch instead of his bed so he can wake up to go to work.

High-arousal children, on the other hand, are immediately in the high range upon waking. Jesse was a high-arousal child. We made a rule that he was not allowed out of his room until it was daylight. He had to play quietly until then. At daylight, he would come into my room, stand very close to my face, and scream, "MOM, IT'S DAYLIGHT—CAN WE GET UP NOW!" Talk about a wake-up call. These children do not do as well on stimulant medication, because it makes them more hyperactive—or, as I call it, "I can't scrape them off the ceiling." Jesse responded better with clonidine (an old blood-pressure medication) that helped lower him off the ceiling.

Children with sensory defensiveness have difficulty getting dressed (tolerating textures/clothes) in the mornings/evenings. They may be picky eaters and have to tolerate eating, standing in line next to a child with ADHD, getting bumped; tolerating the loud noises of school and lunch lines; tolerating a loud intercom, school bell, or buzzer, and so on. They are tolerating, tolerating, tolerating the day-to-day activities that end up looking like high arousal.

Although they look no different from the other children, these children need to be treated for the sensory defensiveness (sensory discrimination disorder). Typically, this treatment is a brushing program. Although many professionals are trained in some version of brushing, I have found the most effective is the Patricia Wilbarger and Julia Wilbarger method. With this, we take a surgical brush (the kind doctors use to wash their hands) and brush the arms, legs, and back. (This is like a deep-tissue massage.) We follow the brushing with joint compressions, pushing in on the joints in a specific way. (This is like a heavy work out with weights). We never brush the stomach area due to possibility that the vagus nerve will cause nausea. We never brush the face, since we cannot control the input, but a child may brush his or her own face. If you are interested in this, find a therapist trained in the brushing method. It is important that it is followed and monitored. Although a very simple method, it is still a therapeutic intervention and should be followed by a therapist. This is a powerful tool in helping children improve.

As a parent, I felt empowered to help my child. When Jesse entered early intervention, I and several therapists were attending different sensory workshops. We used Jesse as our test subject. He was the first to have the brushing program in our early intervention unit. Jesse was easily overloaded. When company would come to see us, Jesse would body slam them as a way of saying hi. We knew the brushing would help Jesse, so we got everyone involved, including his caregiver, since he needed to be brushed every two hours except when he was sleeping

I was at a sensory integration workshop with his occupational therapist, Ms. Sarah. I went home for lunch and Jesse came up to me very nicely and was telling me all about something. (At this time, he only spoke vowels, so he sounded like Jodi Foster in the movie *Nell*). I noticed he was playing nicely for longer periods of time. I honestly thought he was sick. I went back to the workshop and told his therapist. She asked, "How long have we been doing the brushing?" I told her it had been two weeks. She stated, "We are seeing the changes." We did the older version, which was to brush for six weeks and then reduce the frequency of brushing. Although it is a simple technique, it is hard to put into the routine, so we did it for only five weeks.

Over the years I have found that change in language occurs in the first few weeks. If there is some language, you get more output, or if there is more language, you get a better quality (length of conversation, quality, etc.). This is not a magical cure, although it feels like it. The language improves because the body already has the language, but it has been disorganized. Once the brain is able to regulate, the children are able to access the language. At week three or four, you get an improvement in attention and regulation. The child can focus longer on tasks and is more organized with play. At week five to six, you have a different child. The child is more normal in developmental skills, regulation, and expression of emotion. It seems such a simple technique, yet it can have significant changes.

There are other ways to help sensory defensiveness and many books and articles have been written on sensory issues. Article *What is Sensory Integration* by Justin Jensen August 2010 by Prezi; *The Everything Parent's guide to Sensory Integration Disorder,* by Terri Mauro; *Answers to Questions Teachers Ask about Sensory Integration*, by Jane Koomar, Carol Kranowitz, Stacey Szklut, Lynn Balzer-Martin, and others; *Starting Sensory Integration Therapy*, by Bonnie Arnwine; or *The Sensory-Sensitive Child,* by Karen A. Smith and Karen R. Gouze are just a few of the books out there. My most recommended book is *The Out-of-Sync Child,* by Carol Kranowitz, and the follow-up books she has written.

Points on Children's Behaviors

- Children who have poor regulation on the inside will have poor regulation flexibility, which can lead to explosive behaviors. These children have difficulty with transitions, such as going to school, coming home from school, leaving one place to go to another, or changes in routine.

- Children sometimes have extreme irritability or frustration for no apparent reason. When you investigate the reason, you may find intolerance to things in the environment.

- When children are so rigid in their behaviors, families sometime go to extremes to accommodate them. Families will change routines, alter travel plans, etc. in order to maintain peace.

- Children may have poor self-concept or find it difficult to make friends or to be part of a group.

- A child may exhibit aggressive behaviors or be a loner.

- There may be an overreaction or under reaction to pain.

- A child may show poor planning of movement so may be clumsy or not want to engage in physical play. He or she may have poor balance and fall often.

- You may see behaviors that repeat in frequency or intensity, or last longer than typical play (making repetitive sounds, being stuck on video games, etc.).

- The person may be disorganized and lack purpose in activities. She may lack variety in play activities.

- The "good baby" is also a concern, since there could be lack of muscle tone for movement and crying. This is a sensory issue as much as hyperactivity in a child is.
- The person has difficulty calming himself after physical activity or emotional upset.
- Children may be what I call "furniture movers." Some children seek out excessive amounts of sensory input. The climb objects, push furniture around, hang upside, seem "on the go," etc.
- Some children have sensory defensiveness. Their stress cycle, or the "fight, flight, or fright" reaction to sensory input, is turned on. This can occur with any sensory input: tactile, auditory, visual, or an excess of movement (vestibular insecurity).
- Your child may have learning or developmental delays.
- There may be a significant prenatal or birth history.
- There may be a loss of a sense (sight, hearing, etc.), with some of the following associated problems or sensory issues:
- Children may have food or seasonal allergies. Mykel had extreme reactions.)
- Children may have constant or reoccurring ear infections. (Jesse suffered these from the age of one month till over two years of age.)
- Low muscle tone in the mouth or sensory defensiveness can lead to poor eating habits—possibly oral-motor issues.
- Many children with sensory issues have sleep irregularities. (Both my boys still have issues.)

■ Poor regulation of emotions can result in high anxiety and emotional insecurity (Mykel)

■ Because the autonomic system controls the gut there may be problems with digestion and elimination (Jesse)

Sensory Diet
How We Treat Children

(Sensory Diet—this is not food related but is lifestyle change. The sensory diet was developed by Patricia Wilbarger and Julia Wilbarger in their book *Sensory Defensiveness in Children Aged 2–12*)

As a therapist, I have set up many sensory diets for children and their families. I have also lived this as well. Sensory diets, or lifestyles, are about helping children maintain balance and regulation through activities and breaks throughout the day. This process allows more choices (feasting) rather than being a diet that limits. It works best when the family, school, caregivers, and extended family are working together. The focus is to make everyone's lives better, while supporting the child's ability to learn self-regulation. When you understand the sensory concepts and begin living the changes, you will no longer think the way you used to. You will begin spotting the children with dysregulation every time you go to Walmart or a restaurant. We never went out in public without two adults. That way, if one of children would become too overstimulated, an adult could take him to the car.

Our boys had a barrel in which we cut a hole in the side and padded the inside. Their daycare used a wooden box large enough for a child to sit inside. Both were places to go to calm down. This is different than "time out." We called ours the "calm spot"; you could name it what you like (quiet time, chill-out place, etc.). The child learns to go and calm down in a more enclosed place that mimics being tucked in as a baby. Many children have naturally found a spot like this in their homes. They may go under the kitchen table, behind a couch, in the bottom of their closet, or under a desk. All these options can work and can be made into a calm spot with pillows, heavy blankets, headphones, books, etc.

We used the brushing technique. We also increased textural play such as a sandbox, rice or beans in a bucket, water play, etc. We started daily physical play. If it was bad weather outside, we would make an inside obstacle course with chairs and couch cushions and work on prepositions like *over, under, through,* etc. We added "heavy work" with tug-of-war, gardening, and carrying groceries in. My favorite was watching my huge two- to three-year-old Jesse (forty pounds, and forty inches tall) pull his therapist around as she sat in a wagon. We added heavier blankets at night to help him sleep and added a weighted vest at times. Mostly, we learned to keep the routine consistent, as our children did not tolerate change well. This was difficult in a military life, with their father coming and going over and over. I had to become the main rule and routine keeper, and Dad had to learn to ease back into our lives rather than jump in and help after being gone for months. We will talk more about the specific activities for each sensory area later on, but the overall sensory diets should include the following strategies:

■ **Provide a calming, enclosed place** to limit sensory input when a child is overstimulated—a box, under a desk, behind a chair, or in a quiet corner. (Add calming things to this area, such as books, calming music, things to bite on like the Ps and Qs chew toys, or anything that feels right for your child. Remember, it is about the child's way to calm down.)

■ **Use treatments as recommended by a therapist trained in sensory work.** This might include a brushing program (it works like a massage and heavy workout every two hours to shut down the stress cycle and teaches the brain how to function without the stress cycle turned on), use of massage, or use of tactile play with different textures or sensory items.

■ **Use heavy work,** such as lifting and stacking cans, helping bring in groceries, playing with heavy or weighted toys, pushing wheelbarrows, moving furniture, playing outside, climbing ropes, or using playground equipment.

■ **Stay active,** using sports, walking, swimming and, for older children, weight-lifting.

■ **Tactile play,** including water play; Play-Doh; buckets with beans, rice, or sand; paints; whipped-cream play; or toys with textures.

■ **Activities** like pulling heavy items on a blanket, tug-of-war, tumbling, swimming, jumping, etc.

■ **Use of weighted items,** like a heavy blanket, weighted backpack, or weighted vest (monitored by therapist).

My favorite suggestion to families that are overwhelmed when taking their child out in public, especially shopping, is to use a baseball cap (or better yet, a weighted baseball cap), sunglasses, and a backpack that has a few water bottles in it for weight. This helps makes the muscles and joints work and blocks some of the visual stimulation. Pair this with offering something to chew on or a snack that is crunchy, tart, or sour. You will find what works best for your child.

Remember to take only short trips out, and if you can, take an additional person, so they can go to the car with the child when the child gets overwhelmed. We learned this quickly after many disastrous trips out. We would only get through a few aisles in Walmart, Sam's, or Target before our children would fall apart (usually in the electronics aisle, so it was not about toys). My husband would pick the child up, throw him over his shoulder, and walk out, laughing, as everyone watched. You have to get over your embarrassment at others watching you. This is about your child, not whether people think you're doing a good job as a parent. At the car, the child would calm down. (Mainly this was Mykel.)

Our worst episode occurred when I was with my friend Kathy at a local grocery store. Mykel was getting overwhelmed in the store, but he did okay until we were in the checkout line. Then he saw those dreaded toy machines. He wanted a certain toy from the machine. I explained that he would not get to select that toy but that he would get whatever toy came out. When a different toy came out, Mykel lost it. He cried and fell to the floor. I told him he could calm down and take the toy, or we would leave it and go. He yelled that he didn't want it, so I put the toy on top of the machine and proceeded to walk out.

Mykel realized that he was not getting a toy. He then raised the outburst up about three levels and started screaming at the top of his lungs and trying to hit me. Everyone in the parking lot was now looking at me. Kathy was quickly getting Jesse into the vehicle. I was trying to put my fighting child into his side of the car. At this point, he planted his feet on either side of the door, refusing to get in. I got him in, closed the door, and walked around the vehicle several times. Mykel was still screaming. I got in and said, "When you are calm, we will leave."

This was one of those moments when you have to stay consistent. You pick the battle, and you need it in some way to end successfully. As soon as Mykel had to gasp for a few breaths and wasn't screaming, I said, "Thank you for calming down. We are going now." Starting the car quickly, I headed to the road. Before we left the parking lot, Mykel was asleep! This was an example of sensory upset at its finest. When a child is so dysregulated that he can have an outburst like that and then a minute later be asleep, this lets you know how unbalanced his system is. The child gets so overwhelmed that the body shuts down.

I worked with a little boy that had been exposed to drugs in utero. His brain was so disorganized that when he would bump into things, the pain would trigger a seizure, and sometimes he would stop breathing. So if you see a child upset in public who in a few minutes is asleep, you can say to yourself, "That's a sensory issue."

The Goal of Changing Children's Behaviors

The hope in changing behaviors is to enrich children's lives, not limit them. I have parents start at the point where their children are functioning. Usually families have made all kinds of adaptations in order to work around this child. They may have limited their family visits and outings and changed the family routine. We start where the children are, but we want to give families back their lives—possibly better.

We focus on self-regulation, self-calming, sleep, and ways to communicate their needs. We emphasize social skills and regulation with siblings and peers. We work on improving family regulation, and we try new experiences.

Adult Activities

Adults who are dysregulated fill our work environments, schools, and prisons. As adults, we naturally seek out ways to regulate ourselves, usually in relationship systems. We call friends up to gripe about our family members. We fight with others when we are overloaded. We become obsessed. We get stuck on things we think need to occur a certain way. We get frustrated and quit our jobs. We file for divorce when we can no longer tolerate each other. We naturally seek solace in food, drinks, sex, and new relationships. Some adults find healthy outlets, like prayer lives, meditation, exercise, and balanced relationships.

Jesse has recently started college. Because of his sensitivity to others, we were concerned that dorm life would be overwhelming. We encouraged him to get a roommate and have the "college experience" of making friends, staying up late, etc. As God knew best, Jesse's roommate did not come to college. Jesse still made a great effort. He met many people and was very popular quickly. Into the second week, the interaction with so many people caused him to come crashing down. Jesse had to learn to use his room as his "calm place." He rearranged the furniture, made a meditation place, and began using his time effectively so that he had down time during the day.

As an adult, Mykel still has issues with dysregulation. He continues to get overwhelmed, and he withdraws often. The difference now is that he has an understanding of what is happening and is able to choose different options. Mykel uses his "man cave" and sitting around his fire pit as his way of regulation. Here are some activities that help with regulation for adults:

- **exercise**
- **sports such as swimming**
- **relationship systems** (We talk, fight, or have sex to deal with the frustrations of life.)
- **breathing exercises**
- **massage**
- **meditation**
- **prayer**

Spiritual Purpose

After twenty-five years of working with biological parents, foster parents, and their children, I understand that there is purpose in all that happens in life. Jesse has related to me four fundamental laws:

Everything has purpose, even the dark or light.

Everything is equal, no matter how big or small.

God is love, love above all.

God is will—free will. I am will.

Jesse is writing a book about these laws, and I will leave it to him to explain more. I am stating them here as a way to explain to parents the purpose behind the struggle. People often said to me, "Oh it's amazing that you work with this, and then have boys like this." I often wondered why—when you do not have a break, since it is a day-and-night job. Over the years, I began to understand more as to the course of my life's work and why I did have these two amazing children.

I worked close to ten years in the early intervention program in our state (and continued in this area with different agencies). The state program provided services to children with special needs from birth to three years. I started at the beginning of the program, and there was a learning curve. We truly did not understand what we were doing in the beginning. I just knew that when I would swing the children with autism, they would talk. So, every session, we would swing. Some wonderful occupational and physical therapists taught me that vestibular (swinging) movement helped organize children so they could communicate better. Thank God for the people he placed in my life so I could learn.

One of the things that the staff struggled the most with was grieving parents. As outsiders looking in, it was easy to say "Oh, your child has this diagnosis, and we need to do one, two, three ..." Parents would fight, resist, or sabotage treatment at times, and the staff would have a hard time understanding why this was happening. For parents who have children with special needs or behavioral issues, grief becomes a brick wall. The more you try the direct approach to these parents, the more you beat your head against the wall. Sometimes, if you come around the wall and sit with the parents, hold their hands, and wait for them, the wall will begin to crumble. Grief is sometimes processed with others that we trust to show our heartache. These parents grieve the loss of the dream of the healthy child. They grieve the idea of the life they thought they would have. They grieve the loss of family and friends who don't know how to help and do not understand the frustration and pain the parent is suffering.

David struggled with grief when I told him we needed to refer Jesse for our early intervention services. I had tested kids who qualified for services who were talking more than Jesse. I knew we needed more help. When I told him that night, he said, "No there is nothing wrong with Jesse. He is not like Mykel." (No one could deny the difficulty we had with Mykel). David went through a series of emotions that night, including anger, frustration, hurt, and denial. He spoke with his family, who also stated that maybe Jesse needed help; he was really frustrated. Then Jesse did something that reminded him of how Mykel acted. He turned around and said, "Oh my God—they are alike!" He finally saw Jesse's struggle also. Until that moment, no one could have convinced David that Jesse needed help.

To the parents that I worked with and to the parents reading this book, I say, "I know the pain. I know what it is like to face the loss of the dream that you will have a healthy child. I know what it is like to have to give up on your own expectations and dreams for this child. I know how it is when you want so much for him and then are slapped back to reality." I also learned in the process that I was able to release what I had wanted for my children, which in turn let them be whom they were supposed to be, not conforming to my vision. This may have been a great gift, although it was hard to deal with at the time.

There is no shame in grief. If you allow God—spirit, the universe—to help you, those that you need will be placed in your path. You are going through these life choices for a reason. I do not believe that any childhood illness or disability is a punishment from God. My God is a loving God. I do believe we have life lessons and choices. We are presented with struggles so we can choose to learn those lessons and grow or go through them again in some form or fashion.

I look back at my life in reference to the four laws Jesse has taught me. I know my purpose no matter whether times are dark or light—I was put here to shine God's light to others. I have been blessed with the opportunity to meet thousands of children. I feel honored at each encounter. I know that everything is equal, from the doctors to the waitress who helped Jesse feel special—all is equal. I feel humble sitting with a family struggling to cope. I am especially honored to be present at a birth or at a death. Those are sacred moments. All are equal. I know that God is love. Love is the key. Love is what Dr. Grubb and all the physicians we have encountered showed to Jesse. Love is what breaks down the walls of grief. Love is what occurs when a child begins making progress because adults in their life say, "I'm here and present with you."

I also know that God's way is free will, and when our free will and His align, then we are doing our life's purpose and it is for the higher good. When I learn and improve and share that with others, then we all do better. Our higher selves and collective consciousness rises up. This is important, because it is what will help us reach a greater connection with the higher power.

This is the information provided by Jesse on this subject:

"Our spirit (soul) is connected to God (higher power) at all times. Our spirit resides in the body, but the body is just the vessel for the soul. The body systems are made to gather information. They gather the information through many processes. For example, the eyes record everything, like a constant video camera. Every image received is stored in the memory center. Every sound heard by the ear is also remembered. This is apparent when we remember the past. The past is more easily remembered by visual means, like watching a movie, than it is by other senses, like hearing. Only when the senses interact do memories come out properly and complete. This applies to all senses. Every sense is designed to record different information. Power is distributed equally between the senses, in most cases. In cases where one sense is impaired or not functional, the memory will be contained more in another sense. Thus, a blind man may remember more sounds from a party than a sighted man would. Different senses can make up for one that is lacking at that moment. It is the intelligence of the spirit to use them effectively in different situations.

When the spirit/soul gains control of the body and they work together, the spirit/soul will see the majesty of God. The body can see Him in physical form, and the spirit will see Him in the energy form, and both together will see Him in full. This is the ultimate purpose of our next progression— to be one with God. The purpose of science is to learn how the body functions in order to increase our awareness of self and spirit. The physical and spiritual body working together demonstrates joy and peace, which is of God.

CHAPTER 3

Taste: Oral-Motor (Suck, Swallow, Breathe, or SSB: Five Senses)

Medical Definition

Taste: the ability to sense sweet, sour, bitter, and salt within your mouth. Taste buds and your nerve endings send chemical signals to the brain. It also involves the sense of smell, as this is connected.

Oral means "mouth" and *motor* means "movement." Together they mean the ability to use the muscles in the mouth for feeding, speech production, and regulation.

One of my favorite books is the *Out of the Mouths of Babes* by Frick, Oetter, and Richter. I have bought many copies of this book over the years and given them away to parents. The authors have a great way of explaining the process of suck, swallow, breathe (SSB) and how it affects regulation, transition to activities, muscle tone, learning, etc. SSB helps to organize information from the world, and it is the reason babies mouth objects. They are learning about the world around them. SSB helps with growth and development, not only in taking in nourishment but also in motor planning, especially with the use of the hands. Have you ever seen children learn to write? Their mouths are open and sometimes drooling. The hands and mouth are what we call "the triangle." They work together for fine motor tasks such as writing, eating, and completing tasks using the hands. (Gross-motor tasks use larger muscles, such as the legs, for walking) My husband and both children have horrible handwriting. None of them like to write anything. Jesse had occupational therapy until high school. Eventually, the therapist said that there wasn't anything that they could do to help him. Here are some basic points from *Out of the Mouth of Babes*: (Frick and Richter, 1996)

- The timing and interaction of SSB are available at birth to help eat and calm. When babies have birth issues, this can be delayed.
- SSB contributes to increasing muscle strength for moving to solid foods, crying, cooing, and babbling. Lower muscle tone will often limit food selection (soft foods only) as well as sound production ("good" babies).
- SSB plays a part in holding up the head, reaching, grasping, and standing erect.
- Mouth and hands are the "triangle" and are interconnected by cranial nerves. They work together for learning tasks. When a child is doing homework or pencil-and-paper tasks, having something to chew on helps with learning.
- SSB muscles assist in maintaining the health and function of the ears, eyes, and respiratory system. SSB has a spiraling effect in development

Layman's Terms

We look at the mouth as more than the organ to taste food. Our mouth helps us learn about objects. We also look at how we use our muscles in our mouths, what we call oral-motor work. This affects our ability to eat, manage our saliva, and keep our tongues inside our mouths. Our mouths can help us focus—picture adults chewing on pens, smoking, drinking, or eating to keep awake and focus.

Oral-motor system:

- helps us keep alert, calm, and focused
- supports precision and skills
- adds strength and stability for power
- alerts us to potential problems when there is atypical development

The mouth is connected to the cranial nerves and is used from the time we are born until we die. Think about babies taking a bottle, kids sucking on their shirts, adults smoking or chewing a pen—these are all ways we use our mouths to help regulate us. When you watch someone do a difficult task, you sometimes see the person moving her mouth or sticking her tongue out.

Jesse has had fine-motor difficulties throughout his life. Although he could do detailed things with his hands, writing was frustrating. It was like a traffic jam or shorted wire when it came time for him to write. He would drool, keep an open-mouth pose, and write slowly, with much difficulty. Jesse could do elaborate fine-motor tasks such as making creatures. When he was young, he made his "guys" out of paper. I would walk in and there would be paper strips everywhere. If I stepped on one, Jesse would exclaim, "That's the left foot." To us it was strips of paper, but to him it was his masterpiece. He later made creatures out of pipe cleaners. They had weapons, powers, and names. It was his entire world. All along he used his mouth when working on such detailed objects. We learned to offer lots of chewing options for Jesse while he did fine-motor tasks.

I also like to add here that although children with sensory issues may have trouble tolerating their environment, for the most part they are bright, creative children. It has been a joy to watch their problem-solving and creative solutions.

Children's Behaviors

Children begin oral-motor work with the bottle. They use their mouths from their childhood into adulthood to help with regulation. Children mouth toys as a way of exploration and learning. Children suck on bottles, pacifiers, and other objects as a way of calming. Children will have their hair in their mouths, will suck on their shirts, or will bite something as a way of concentrating when learning to write. Adolescents use extreme drinks and snacks as a way of dealing with stress. Snacks that are sour, sweet, salty, or spicy are ways children and adults regulate their bodies using the mouth for input. Into adulthood, people continue to use chewing on pens, biting, overeating, drinking, and smoking as ways to calm themselves.

Sensory Activities

My favorite section of the *Out of the Mouths of Babes* book is the Oral-Motor Grocery List that gives ideas for oral stimulation. Mykel had very low arousal and was hard to wake up, so we would do some of these types of activities.

- Use touch, firm pressure, and nice pats on the back to wake him.
- Offer tart juice, such as cranberry or orange juice while Mykel was getting ready. (Even as an adult, Mykel loves juice to this day.)
- Have his choice of clothing ready (and yes, I did let him pick it out, but it had to be ready the night before, so there was less fussing in the morning). My family still teases me for the "riggings" my children wore. They were always tying some rope or strap to themselves.
- Hum, sing, and make up songs, which were goofy at times, to keep my boys laughing and not fussing. Both boys had difficulty with eating certain textures of food.
- Fifteen to twenty minutes before eating, engage in activities that promoted sucking, blowing, biting, crunching, and chewing. These included blowing cotton balls down the table with straws, blowing whistles and flutes, blowing bubbles in the air or in

liquid, crunching ice, playing puffy cheeks, blowing raspberries, smacking lips, or singing silly songs

Adult Behaviors

The boys watched themselves as children on home movies, and they laughed about themselves drooling while learning to walk. Mykel admitted that even today he has his mouth open if he is trying to write. Mykel does not like writing, because it is difficult and he knows that he has to have his mouth open. Jesse told us that when he writes or works with his hands he still chews on his shirt. I have witnessed his shirt being soaked on many occasions, even now that he is an adult.

Mykel stated that he has issues with temperature of foods and must heat things up. He cannot eat cold pizza or even cold sandwiches. Our friend Kathy is the same way; she hates to get food to go, because she would rather eat it hot. She also had to learn to eat food, like stew, that had many different textures. She does not eat berries or bananas, due to seeds. (Yes, bananas have tiny seeds you can see when you slice them lengthwise.)

Spiritual Purpose

Jesse has stated the following:

"In all major religions and health, the breath of life is an essential element. God gives us the breath of life as the soul enters the body. The most complicated mechanism is the ability to breath. Our souls do not need to breath. So when they incarnate, the soul must learn to breathe. The breath becomes the body's flow. Just as all things flow through the body with the breath, so does change. The reason the skill of breathing is necessary is to keep balance and heal the body through the breath of life. It is a sign of distress when the body is not in balance. The breath will shape the body and all functions, including that of the brain. Those who forget the breath are the ones that stop change. The breath allows the body to become an open channel to connect with spirit/ higher power. The air that is breath is the best representation of the one true God, invisible, but only known by those who believe."

When I am working with children on self-regulation, we begin with breathing, relaxation techniques, sometimes meditation, and calming techniques using the mouth. These are the easiest for young children to learn but are also critical for all humans to understand. You can literally affect all your vital signs by deep breathing. You can balance your oxygen and carbon dioxide levels in your brain with 4x4 breathing (breathe in for count of four, hold for a count of four, then breathe out for a count of four, and hold for a count of four).

How powerful is the breath of life! How liberating is it to find your voice when you learn to speak. God has given life through the breath. He expects us to find our voices and to be the helpers of others—through our uplifting words, not through the destruction of them. How will you use your breath?

CHAPTER 4

VISION (FIVE SENSES)

Medical Definition

Our visual system is very involved. As a camera or camcorder does, the human eye takes in light by the retina. The retina has light-sensitive nerve cells called cones and rods. The rods secrete rhodopsin to help us see in the semidarkness. Cones help us see objects in bright light. The area where the optic nerve goes through the retina has no cones or rods; it is called the blind spot. The interesting part is that the optic nerve from the left and right eyes meets at the optic chiasma. The nerve exits and transfers impulses from the left eye to the left visual center in the cerebral cortex, and the impulses for the right side are transferred to the right. The brain takes the two halves and makes one picture. What is amazing is how the brain can fill in missing information. This image is inverted due to the light refracting when it is perceived by the retina. We do not know how the brain converts the image upright.

Vision is considered as the perception of form, color, size, movement, and distance of objects.

Important Facts on Vision:

- Eight percent of information we take in is through vision.
- Two-thirds of brain activity is devoted to vision when the eyes are open.
- Eighty to ninety percent of human communication is nonverbal, of which fifty five percent comes from seeing the speaker's facial expressions and body gestures.
- Seventy five to ninety percent of classroom learning depends on vision.
- Vestibular and proprioceptive systems profoundly influence vision.
- Many visual problems are never diagnosed or treated.
- Twenty five percent of all school-age students have undiagnosed vision problems.
- Seventy percent of juvenile delinquents have undiagnosed vision problems.
- Vision issues with children who have autism include differently shaped rods and cones in the eyes. Their vision is better from the side than the front, hence their poor eye contact.

Layman's Terms

So much of our social interaction is based on visual input. Some days we are bombarded with visual input. Stores stack items high up on shelves, and nonstop television, video games, billboard signs, and bright flashing signs provide constant visual movement. These items can easily overload children who have sensory issues.

We have to look at visual input in several ways. There are the functional aspects of the eyes, and there is the aspect of how the input is processed. Then we have to consider how overwhelming visual input can become. It is mandatory in the foster-care system to have the children checked for hearing and visual issues. So many of our children have visual issues that greatly affect learning. Think about a school setting—most of the teachers uses the visual and auditory system. Teachers use visual aids and give verbal instructions. Learning is directly affected if either of these systems is deficient.

Children's Behaviors

Children have many types of learning, and it is important to find out what learning type your child uses. This helps to customize the learning experience for your child. I have learned that most young children are experiential learners. The more sensory input they have, the better they retain the information. For example, if they could see, feel, hear, and do something with an object/concept, then they will retain the information. Mykel was a kinesthetic (or movement) learner. He had to *do* the task to understand it. When he had to learn his address, he struggled with just memorizing the information. We would take him to the street sign and then to the numbers on the house, and then we would have Mykel say the address. The day he was able to state his address on his own, he ran outside, looked up at the house numbers, and was able to remember the entire address.

Visual learners will be discussed in detail in the section on autism. Children with autism learn almost everything with the visual system. Children with autism take in visual information all at once—even the things that need to be screened out, which can be overwhelming. We may walk into a room and be able to focus on someone talking, while screening out the light flickering or the hum of a ceiling fan. Children with autism take in all that information at the same level as the person talking. It can be overstimulating and can cause behavioral outburst simply due to the environment. Children with autism also learn all the details of visual information. They pay attention to details that most of us easily dismiss.

When children become overwhelmed with visual input, parents can limit the input. At home or school, turning off lights can instantly calm an environment. Having kids wear sunglasses or hats can limit input.

Sensory Activities

My boys loved visual learning games. At night, we especially liked playing with flashlights and Hacky Sacks and catching lightning bugs. The boys loved the trampoline the best. We would write letters randomly, in chalk, on the trampoline. The boys would work on their spelling words by jumping to the different letter, such as jumping from C to A to T.

Other Visual Activities

- play flashlight tag
- play balloon volleyball, Hacky Sack, or catch with sensory balls or beanbags
- dance with scarves or capes or pieces of fabric
- turn off lights when a child is overwhelmed
- use mazes, tracing, lacing cards, connect-the-dots, etc.
- trace letters on someone's back or carpet squares, or chalk on a trampoline
- blow bubbles, play board games, flash laser lights, etc.

Adult Behaviors

Mykel and Jesse both became addicted to video games due to the games' ability to constantly change. Although this held the boys' short attention, in the long run it did not improve their attention; in fact, it worsened their attention. The boys as adults still need lots of visual input to keep their attention. Both boys stated that they still get easily overwhelmed by lots of visual stimulation. Both still have addictions to video games. They both report problems with tolerating bright lights. I have issues with fluorescent lights myself. At my center, the children with autism would always tell me when the bulb was going out before it started flickering. These lights give me a headache from the magnetic field that extends down from them. Many schools cover the lights with softening materials, but this will not be enough if this is an issue for your child.

Spiritual Purpose

Jesse has always had spiritual sight. These are his thoughts on his gifts. "Spiritual sight is a skill that must be practiced. The sight is a triad of parts: the sight of the physical eyes, the sight of the spiritual eyes, and the sight of the energy eyes. Then there is the sight of the physical, spiritual, and energy heart.

"Spiritual sight comes from the soul's ability to see things further into the dimensional range. This is the sight that you see when you close your eyes. Spiritual sight only works with the spiritual heart in tandem with the spiritual eyes. This allows the sight to see and notice the souls around it. This is the sense you are using when you feel that someone is watching you.

"There is also the ability to see energy. This comes from the body's own energy field. The energy field is able to detect the flow of energy around it. It is able to determine the direction, form, and shape of the energy. When you only use the body's energy sight, spirits will appear as shapeless forms or shadows. When all the parts of sight work together, the physical is the anchor, the energy will discern whether something is there, and the spiritual will determine the detail of the object or energy. To open this gift, it is necessary to focus on seeing things in a deeper way than you did before. You must see connection to people as tethers that cannot be broken. You must focus on the reason behind things and the inner qualities rather than the outward appearance or assumed actions. The power of sight is determined by your strength of the heart. Seeing the truth is a greater weapon than any that has existed.

"With patience comes peace, which then becomes sight beyond words. Connecting with spirit and finding the stillness opens the inner sight. Sight holds power beyond that of a picture. Pictures are only one instant of the past. They can only show you what is behind you. Video is the same. You cannot look behind; you must look forward (it's why our eyes are in front of us). The only moment you have is now, but the future is shaped with your will. Nature is aware of the fact that *now* is all that is."

The brain has two of every structure, one on the right and one on the left, except for the pineal gland. There is only one pineal gland. This gland actually has rods and cones (the photoreceptors of the eyes) and is wired to the visual cortex. The pineal gland is a pea-sized gland in the center of the brain. The label comes from Latin *pinea*, meaning "pinecone." Pinecone symbols were used for psychic or spiritual signs. Major religions have used this symbol for spiritual sight; Edgar Casey and others have stated that the function of the pineal gland is to enable our spiritual sight. It is thought that the gland could also pick up sound vibration using cells called pinealocytes. Many believe this is the gland responsible for spiritual sight or the "third eye." This is, of course, not to be feared, as God has designed our bodies with these abilities. These abilities are to be used, and we will learn more about the body's functions as science continues to investigate these areas.

The HeartMath project, founded by Doc Childre, has spent over twenty years researching the heart's connection to our energetic fields. Research has determined that the heart actually radiates an electrical field around the body. We will discuss this more in detail in the Heart section. We believe that spiritual sight and intuition are connected to this heart-intuitive intelligence. Spiritual sight has more to do with an open heart and willingness to see what God has for you.

For our family, this has been a very long journey. Jesse's gifts prompted much learning for us. We grew up with little experience of these gifts. It was unusual for us to watch Jesse communicate what he could see or share the wisdom of what might happen. Many family members did not believe in his gifts. His father struggled with trying to see how Jesse could help others. He did not know how this fit into his religious beliefs.

All I knew was that I believed in my son and needed to understand how to support him. I began educating myself. God placed many wonderful people in our path, and this helped Jesse develop more of his gifts. Jesse has helped me strengthen my own beliefs that we are all capable of spiritual sight and God is waiting on us to be open to His glory. For other parents with children like Jesse, I say this: Please allow them this expression, help them not be afraid, help them learn protection, and most of all, believe them.

Chapter 5

Auditory (Five Senses)

Medical Definition

Sound is recorded as waves, which can be measured on a graph; the wave unit is measured as frequency in hertz (Hz). Sound in air travels 340 meters per second. The human ear can respond in the range of 20 Hz to 20,000 Hz. The ear structure consists of the outer, middle, and inner ear. Most people have seen the drawing of the ear structure at the doctor's office. The ear consists of the outer ear, the pinna (ear we see), and the ear canal. The middle ear has the eardrum, which separates the outer ear from the middle ear. It consists of a tympanic membrane that vibrates with sound.

There are three bone structures forming the ossicles: the malleus, the incus, and the stapes. These sit in the oval window that separates the middle ear from the inner ear. The middle ear is connected with the back of the throat through the Eustachian tube. In children, this tube is more parallel or level with the ground so it does not drain well down the back of the throat. The tube tilts downward as we get older. This is the reason you should not lay down a baby with a bottle; the fluid can cause ear infections. The inner ear has two parts, the vestibular system and the cochlea (which looks like a seashell spiral). Hair-cell receptors are a very important part of hearing; they are called corti. The corgi responds to fluid bone vibration with 15,000 to 20,000 auditory nerve receptors on the hair cell. This can be damage by things such as excess or loud noises.

We can pinpoint where a sound is coming from because we have two ears. The auditory nerve takes the information to the brainstem, midbrain, and auditory cortex. This function of interpreting sound is called auditory processing. Auditory processing is the brain's ability to make sense of what the ear has heard. Individuals with auditory processing difficulty take in the sound but, as if they were in a traffic jam, cannot separate the individual sounds. People with auditory processing disorder or central auditory processing disorder (CAPD) may have trouble distinguishing between sounds or have trouble listening to sounds in noisy backgrounds. These children and adults cannot process well the information they hear.

Those with Auditory Processing Disorder (APD) have the following symptoms:

- difficulty paying attention and remembering oral information
- difficulty carrying out multistep directions
- low academic performance: poor spelling, vocabulary, and reading-comprehension skills
- difficulty processing information for example, following directions, developing vocabulary, and understanding language.

Behavioral problems

Key Points on Auditory System

- It is connected with the vestibular sense.
- We can't learn to hear, but we can learn to listen.
- There are four aspects of sound: intensity (loudness), frequency (pitch), duration, and localization.
- Central auditory processing disorder is not same as deafness or hearing loss but is miscommunication in the processing of auditory information.

Layman's Terms

The sensory system for hearing is a complex physical structure of the ears, brain process, and sound itself. We have learned that sound comes as vibration, energy or waves. Many of us have seen a sound-wave chart. This is easy to understand if you have ever thrown a rock into a lake and watched the ripples move outward. This is how sound waves travel.

As the information is translated to the brain, many issues can occur. There can be difficulty with the structures themselves. Jesse has a faulty signal from his brainstem, and it affects one side of his body more than the other. On the left side, his eardrum will not move, which greatly affects how he hears from that side. When we were given this information, after going through all the tests on his heart and dealing with his developmental delays for years, we were not surprised. The audiologist came out very somberly and related the news to us. He stated that the problem was from the brain, and there was no way to fix the issue. We looked at each other, laughed, and told him, "We already know all about the spot on the brainstem."

After the sound passes the structure of the ear and vestibular system, it must be processed by the brain. This is a difficult thing to understand for some parents; they know the child can hear but he never seems to respond back appropriately. Auditory process is like a busy city freeway at rush hour. Sometimes there is a traffic jam, and nothing seems to move or work right. This is a significant issue with children who are labelled autistic. Their auditory systems are not their strength and should not be the basic form of learning.

Children's Behaviors

Have you ever taken a child into a public bathroom that has the hand dryers, especially the jet-powered ones? If you have a child with sensory auditory defensiveness, then you could have a meltdown on your hands. My boys would run from bathrooms. I have to admit that once, traveling with lots of friends, I did the same when several dryers were going at once.

With auditory issues you can have a defensive reaction (Mykel was always saying, "Dad is talking too loud!") You can also have auditory processing issues: the structures of the ear are working but the information processed by the brain is faulty. This is, of course, a part of the issues of autism spectrum. Autistic children are visual learners, and communication through the auditory sense can be difficult. Mykel had major auditory-processing issues. He would only process 70 percent of what was heard, and with background noises, he then would drop to 30 percent. When we spoke to Mykel, we had to learn to turn off the radio or TV. We would make sure Mykel was looking at us so that he could hear what was said to him. His most difficult times at school were at noon in the lunchroom, when it was time to play outside, and during music time. Can you imagine what it would be like to be a child hearing only 30 percent of the information in a crowded, loud lunchroom?

Sensory Activities

- dancing, homework, drawing, playing to music
- beating rhythm instruments: we use Native American prayer drums; they add an amazing vibration to our prayers
- moving body parts up and down to music, slide whistles, etc.
- jumping rope to music or chants
- Hemi-Sync recordings (www.hemi-sync.com), Mozart for Modulation CDs, or therapies such as auditory integration training
- games such as cake walks, musical chairs, etc.
- teaching children how to limit irritating sounds, such as wearing earplugs, using a white-noise machine, or moving away from loud noises.

Adult Behaviors

Mykel and Jesse today describe hating the high-pitched sound of computers starting up, high-pitched sounds from TV or static noise, and the sounds of tools, saws, mowers, etc. as sounds that bother them. Mykel says he hates the sound a pencil makes as it writes on paper. Mykel also hates the sound of others smacking as they chew (Jesse's poor oral-motor skills and smacking sounds). Mykel cannot be in total silence either, whereas Jesse cannot be in total darkness. Both do not like the loudness of concerts, but that is mainly due to the crowd sound and tolerating the large group of people.

Mykel and Jesse both avoid situations of irritating noise. They have used earplugs to help, but mainly they now just try to "push through it," while telling themselves it will be over soon.

Spiritual Purpose

When we look at the spiritual side of sound, we must begin with vibration. Most people understand that vibration occurs and sound waves travel. The next level is to understand that vibration is like a current of energy. This vibration occurs in our bodies and triggers the release of neuropeptides, which affect our state of well-being. If you can change the frequency of the body, you can create balance. Certain sounds resonate in our bodies, raising our own vibration levels. Think of of Tibetan chants, Native American drumming, meditation chants, spiritual songs, or the Dolby sound played before movies—all can resonant in the body and cause a sensory response.

Practitioners of acupuncture believe the body has meridians that should be kept in balance. Western medicine states that acupuncture primarily produces its effects through regulating the nervous system. Regulation of the nervous system works with endorphins and the immune system. Studies have shown that acupuncture may alter brain chemistry by changing the release of neurotransmitters and neurohormones.

Our family goes to see an incredible healer. She checks our pulses to find the body's imbalances and uses acupuncture needles at certain points to balance our bodies. These are tiny needles, not the long ones seen on television. You only need a few needles; it is not about how many needles you can get. She also checks our chakras to keep them open. (According to Hindu metaphysical belief, chakras are centers in the body where the life force or life energy flows through major plexuses of arteries, veins, and nerves. Chakras are also used in healing modalities.) Our healer uses Reiki energy work to assist the body in higher frequencies and healing. While she works on us, she uses sound to create a calm and balanced environment. She has a Tibetan crystal "singing bowl" that can assist in unblocking meridians and clearing the chakras. She uses tuning forks on the body; this is called sonocytology or vibro-acoustic healing.

Why do certain sounds resonate with our bodies, help our vibration, and balance our meridians and chakras? Higher vibrations are associated with better health, emotional balance, and higher intelligence. Sound vibration waves form patterns known as Fibonacci spirals. When we study physics we learn that Fibonacci spiral patterns appear in nature; they are seen in strawberries, pine cones, pineapples, sunflowers, etc. The patterns consist of spirals that curve in both the "dexter" form (clockwise) and the "sinister" form (counterclockwise). Mathematicians love them, since the numbers of spirals on a surface are two consecutive numbers in the Fibonacci sequence (1, 1, 2, 3, 5, 8, 13, etc.). http://www.physics.org

Sound can affect Fibonacci spirals, raise the level of the body's own vibrations, and affect DNA. The spiral pattern conducts oscillating energy. It occurs in DNA and silicon dioxide, which are two components of all life. Silicon dioxide is the most abundant mineral found throughout the earth's crust. It is also found in vitamin supplements. Silicon dioxide's benefits include preventing arthritis and osteoporosis, and improving the skin, hair, and nails.

Certain sounds, such as a tuning fork, vibrate at the same pitch and rate as a healthy chakra or tissue. Resonance occurs. This opens, strengthens, and clears the chakra, tissues, or organs. Silicon dioxide within the body acts as a conductor, sending the messages on a cellular level. DNA is also sympathetically stimulated. So next time you hear a sound that seems to resonate with your body, pause and listen. Your body will thank you.

Sacred geometry has been used over the years in many kind of religious structures, including altars, tabernacles, churches, mosques, and temples. The geometric shapes can be simple or can be in elaborate patterns. Sound can also form sacred geometric patterns at certain vibrations. This was demonstrated on a popular video, where sand was placed over a speaker; as different sounds were played, the sand formed different sacred geometric shapes. It was originally performed by Hans Jenny in the 1960–1970s. One incredible sound experiment used the sound of *om*, which created a Sri Yantra mandala, which is an ancient geometric form.

Jesse is great at meditation, but my ADHD brain had difficulty with this practice. I have always taught others that prayer is our thoughts being sent to God, invocations were our wills stating what we would do, and meditation was the ability to get quiet and listen to God's response. I'm not good at the listening part. God usually has to use a 2 x 4 upside my head.

Then we found the Wayne Dyer and James F. Twyman meditation CD, *I Am*. It uses turning forks to spell out "I am that I am." This helps create delta waves in the brain. When we started using the CD, for the first two weeks we would both open our eyes at the ten-minute mark. Although there are two twenty-minute tracks, we could not go past that mark. Finally we surpassed it.

CHAPTER 6

TOUCH (FIVE SENSES)

Medical Definition

The touch-sensory system includes touch, temperature, and pain receptors (nociception), and it works with proprioception (body position). The sensory receptors cover the skin, along with muscles, bones, joints, and epithelia. In the medical field, the touch system is referred as a somatic sense. The receptors take in the sense of stimulus through thermoreceptors, nociceptors, mechanoreceptors, and chemoreceptors. The process passes through nerves, into the spinal cord, and into the brain.

Main Points:

- largest sensory system
- main channel during pre-birth and infancy
- provides information on texture, size, shape, and function of object
- measures pressure of touch, vibration, temperature, pain, skin stretch, movement

Layman's Terms

The touch system is easily taught to us when we are young. Children learn early about touch and how information about objects can be related to us. It helps us learn about the world around us. Even when other senses are not functional, such as vision or hearing, touch can compensate and help with learning. The important information to remember is that the touch sense involves not only the texture of an object but also size, shapes, and use of the object. We also understand touch through pain receptors, temperature, vibration, and movement. You can help children with the touch system through texture play but also through pressure, such as wearing biker-type shorts, weighted vests, or heavy blankets.

Children's Behaviors

This story of Mykel has more to do with temperature control, but I had to add it in. Mykel was very tactilely defensive. He only wore cotton clothes and did not tolerate sitting in car seats, where he easily got hot. On hot days, when the car would heat up, he would begin complaining. He would say "Mama, blow me!" This meant turn on the air conditioner. I will never let him live that one down.

As defensive Mykel was to touch (not wanting to be held, not tolerate clothes, avoiding certain textures), he also craved touch, especially soft textures. This I did not understand, because I saw things on a continuum line—children who could not tolerate touch on one end and those that craved it on the other end. An occupational therapist named Teresa told us once that it is more like a circle. Those that are on the far extremes will flip-flop back and forth.

That was Mykel. So, as little as he would tolerate, he was also, at the other extreme, craving touch input. For example, both my boys would consistently climb on me. If I sat down for any length of time, the boys would climb all over me, touching my face and hair. My husband would say, "Quit wallowing all over your mom." But one of the funniest stories of Mykel (yes, I have it on video and show it in my seminars) is when he would rub my friend's legs when she had on knee-high panty hose. One night, he took them off her, and we found him in the dining room in the dark with only his underwear on and her knee highs that went up to his little whitey-tighty underwear. He was prancing around, rubbing his hands up and down his legs. We got the videotape recorder out so he could prance around in front of the camera showing off his "socks." When we asked him whose socks they were, he said, "My daddy's socks." Needless to say, my husband did not think this was funny.

Sensory Activities

- Texture play helps the increase tolerance such as using Play-Doh, goo, and our favorite, cornstarch and water, which seems dry when you play with it and when you stop kneading it becomes more liquid in your hands.
- Any art helps with sensory play as well as creativity: drawing or painting on any surface, including paper,

fences, sidewalks, or paper on walls, which helps with different positions and additional sensory input.

- Exploring different temperatures, such as warm, hot, cool, or cold will help with regulation. Many children love baths to help them regulate.
- Helping in the kitchen can include sensory work with kneading dough, mixing, etc.
- Manipulating Lego, lacing beads or boards, blocks, and—my favorite—using a metal coffee can with different shapes cut into the plastic lid and having the child sort heavy washers, nuts, and bolts can work on fine motor tasks as well as eye hand coordination.
- Playing outside with pine cones, leaves, feathers, sticks, dirt, sand, or water can be sensory play in nature.
- Dressing up with hats, scarves, capes, boots, etch can be rainy day, inside fun.

Adult Behaviors

While I was videotaping the interviews with the boys about their sensory experiences as adults, we noted that both of them sat in the same exact way, with a laid-back position and right hand up by the head. If one changed position, the other would follow and sit in the same way. They were mirroring each other as they spoke—without their awareness, until I brought it up. Mirroring is a behavior humans do when they are becoming connected or in sync with another. It is a technique taught to help people learn to listen and communicate with others.

Mykel described continuing issues with his clothes. He never wears shorts, due to the line around his knee and feeling the fabric. He continues to wear only cotton. He cannot tolerate other textures, saying, "It feels like ants are all over me." Jesse described not being able to tolerate long-sleeved shirts or bulky material.

Mykel and his wife, Elisabeth, discussed the fact that Mykel still has issues with sleeping between sheets. He could never sleep between the sheets, and he and Elisabeth only put bottom sheets on the bed. Elisabeth stated that she has gotten used to sleeping that way. They both use soft comforters instead for covers, and Mykel tends to need his own specific one.

Mykel and Jesse both like sand (we lived on the beach for four years) and remembered my sand and rice bins for texture work. Mykel has to feel soft things at any store but can't stand the feel of cardboard. Mykel says he avoids it but has to open boxes at his work. He hates the sound and feel. Mykel described how after he washes his hands all paper, such as money, receipts, and cardboard, bothers him for a while. Mykel knows he has to work, so he tries to put the irritation to the back of his mind and push through until he is done.

Spiritual Purpose

One of the most spiritual people I know is my aunt Lorene—everyone calls her Granny Barlow. She is one hundred years of age. She has always lived by shining God's light and never judged others for their choices or lifestyles.

She says, "I always talk to God before I put my feet on the ground in the morning, or nothing will go right." If Granny Barlow ever told me "God told me to tell you …," I would have to agree with her. One of the things I noticed about her as her other senses began to fail is that Granny Barlow uses touch to compensate for the loss of sight or hearing. Touch is one of the last senses to fail.

My brother contracted legionnaires' pneumonia and almost died in 2012. Both lungs filled, he had a heart attack, and the worst stage of septic shock—including very low temperature, no arterial blood in his extremities, and all his major organs shutting down. We were told at the first hospital that he was dying, and he was placed on a ventilator. They took him by life-flight helicopter to a critical care unit in Tulsa, Oklahoma.

Both the ER doctor and the critical care unit doctor told the family that he was dying. He was not able to respond to the family, but we used touch and talking to him to communicate. During the next few weeks, we saw so many miracles. First he survived the initial forty-eight to seventy-two-hour period with an incredible group of nurses and doctors working on him. During this time, we were not able to connect with my brother. But Jesse was able to communicate to him.

The first night was the most critical. At this point, I had taken my mother, sister, and Becky, his ex-wife (who had been married to him for twelve years) to the hospital. I had not communicated with Jesse since we'd left, right after John had been put on the helicopter. Jesse had been in school. That evening, we had to leave the hospital room so that a PICC line could be put into John's vein. As we were sitting in the waiting room, Jesse called me. At this point, Jesse knew his uncle John was in the hospital but not what his condition was. Jesse asked if I was with John. I said no, and he told me that I needed to be near him to give him energy. I needed to do some Reiki on him. He began to describe John as having poison in his blood and getting very tired of the fight. He stated that he was giving up and things were shutting down. In reality, John was in septic shock, and all his organs *were* shutting down. Jesse informed me that his next exit point (one of the points in life where the soul may leave) would be Sunday at 3:11 p.m.

I went back into the room and was able to give my brother several Reiki treatments over the next few days. What I learned about this process was how perceptive to touch he was, even through the heavy sedation due to being on a ventilator. John responded to touch—but especially in the loving way Becky cared for him. He was only able to open his eyes briefly and move slightly. I was keenly aware of his soul's presence with us.

On Saturday, he took a turn for the worse. Due to neurological signs, such as his eyes not lining up, lack of response to pain stimulus, etc., they believed he had had a stroke. They did an MRI and worked very hard for the third day in a row. Becky, her sister, and I had many discussions that day, all instinctively about John choosing to die. We finally surrounded his bed, and Becky bravely told him that we wanted him to stay, but if he chose to leave, then we would honor that wish. We released him. I could not see any visual change, but internally I felt an ease in the room.

On Sunday, my sister, cousin, and aunt all came. For the first and only time, Becky left the hospital for a brief time, to go and eat dinner. My aunt and I were the only ones in the room at 2:40 p.m. when my brother started coughing and choking; his vent tube was clogged. As my aunt left the room to go get help, I was overwhelmed with a sense of high vibration surrounding me. I felt a higher vibration, which in turn made my heart rate rise and breathing become shallow. I looked at the clock and thought, *Oh no, here we go!* That feeling stayed with me as the nurse came in to help him, and at this time Becky showed up. There were too many people in the room at the time, but I did not want to leave until after 3:11. Becky was standing at the sink, with her back toward the room (later she told us she had been overwhelmed with a feeling in the room and could not think why she had just been standing there). So I stated out loud, for the nurse's sake, that I was going out to the waiting room, but I packed my stuff up slowly.

The energy was very strong and overwhelming, and I kept saying internally, "John, if you want to go, you can." After 3:11 p.m. the feeling eased, and John's breathing was better. I left the room thinking to myself that being present with someone who died would be very different from now on. A short time later, we went back into the room. My sister was saying goodbye to my brother. She patted him on the arm. He opened his eyes and tracked both eyes over to her. She was surprised and said, "I love you, Bubba." He shook his head to say yes—with intent. We both screamed. From that moment on, things changed quickly. The man that doctors felt would be on dialysis, be on the ventilator for four to six weeks, and have very long recovery—if he lived—soon showed them all wrong. By Tuesday, he ripped his own ventilator out. He was moved from the critical care unit to the cardiac ICU on Thursday, and miracle after miracle began to occur.

On Friday and Saturday, he was having more memory and processing issues. He could not write well; he thought that people were trying to kill him, and he insisted Becky put up a sign that said he was on "auto pilot." Jesse insisted on going to see him. Jesse worked with John, and he helped him understand that it was his will that determined whether he kept his diagnoses. He talked to him about believing that he was completely well. The doctors stopped the morphine that my brother had been receiving. By Sunday, John's kidneys began to function better, his memory and brain function returned, and he was physically up and walking throughout the weekend. The heart doctors were the only ones saying that he had damaged most of his heart and he had a massive blood clot in the middle of his heart that they could do nothing about. By Monday (Christmas Eve), there was no blood clot, and he was released straight out of the cardiac ICU. By the end of January, he was back to work and had a full recovery.

My brother spent most of 2013 in turmoil. He left his ex-wife again, lost his job, and suffered some residual effects from his hospitalization. It was as if his soul did not want to be here anymore. On November 2, 2013, he was found dead in his sleep. No one had had contact with him since October 31. What was interesting is that on October 31 I spoke of him often throughout the day. We had both been adopted on that day, and I had shared many stories of him. In my heart, I believe he died then and my soul already knew this information.

At his funeral, we honored him for the way he had lived. He was the real "Larry the Cable Guy." We put his ashes in a John Deere cookie jar. We sang lots of fun songs like "Chicken Fry" and "Cheeseburger in Paradise." His sisters wrote the eulogy and included "You might be a redneck" jokes. Jesse said that my brother loved it.

Some Native American cultures believe that one soul must die to prepare for a new birth. The soul that leaves brings the new soul here. My youngest sister had two wonderful boys, Randy and Jacob. These boys were active kids, like my sons, but my sister helped her boys through lots of sports. Sports kept her boys regulated. Randy and his wife, Emily, were about to have a child when my brother died. My brother was very excited to have a new baby in the family. Trenton was born a few days after my brother's death. He was born without an anus. He was life-flighted to Children's hospital. Since he was born with a birth defect, he had a colostomy and will endure many reconstructive surgeries. What I watched was all too familiar—the pain and grief on those parents' faces and my nephew saying that he felt helpless to care for his son. His wife was feeling overwhelmed and afraid that she would hurt Trenton.

I also saw the resilience of human nature, and the protectiveness of parents caring for their child. Yes, they wondered why it had happened to them, but they quickly said, "Okay, what do we do now?" The most amazing sight was watching this baby in NICU, on a ventilator, after surgery, being calmed by his father's touch and his voice. That moment was powerful. That moment exemplified love.

CHAPTER 7

SMELL: OLFACTORY (FIVE SENSES)

Medical Definition

Olfactory receptors detect the presence of smell. They come together at the glomerulus. The glomerulus transmits signals to the olfactory bulb, located directly above the nasal cavity and below the frontal lobe.

Main Points about the Olfactory Sense

- It's interconnected with taste: most taste is actually smell.
- Food aversions are a touch issue.
- Smell travels through the limbic system (emotions, memory, pleasure, learning).
- Under sensitivity to taste (e.g., from cigarette smoking) results in excess spices being used in cooking.

Layman's Terms

The sense of smell is closely tied to taste, and since it is tied to the limbic system, it's very closely connected to memory. As I worked with women and children who were sexually abused, I learned how smell can be a trigger to memories of trauma.

We have those memories of sights and smells from our favorite places. We have memories of smells from loved ones' homes or from holidays. When we moved to Biloxi, Mississippi, I sent a box to my sister and two nephews. When they opened it, my nephews were so excited that the box smelled like my home. I did not know my home had a particular smell. When my sister related this story, I said "What does my home smell like?"

She said, "Tide and Downy." I guess the smell of clean is a good smell to have in your home!

Children's Behaviors

Mykel was my sensory-defensive child, so smell was no different. He would walk into a room and say, "What's that smell?" when no one else could smell anything. Smell was overwhelming to him at times. Smell can also trigger nausea, since the senses are tied to the vagus nerve. Many people will get nausea with bad smells. Smell can also be helpful, with aromatherapy options. Smells can help create a calm, tranquil place for resting. Many spas have aromatherapy massages now.

Sensory Activities

Our task was learning to limit smells that triggered the stress cycle for Mykel. He was sensitive to perfumes and strong deodorants. We limited certain cooking smells— frying, beans, cabbage, etc.—by getting a grill with a burner to cook foods outside.

Aromatherapy is based on the belief that smells affect the emotions in the limbic system. If this is an area you are interested in, there are many books and websites that can help you, including www.aromatherapy.com. Lavender and chamomile are usually used to help calm children. There are some wonderful mood blends that help invigorate, relax, or calm, etc.

Adult Behaviors

As with children, adults can learn to avoid those smell issues that cause a strong reaction. Adults can use scents to help create moods in their homes. Mykel and his wife purchased our home, which had been built by my dad. When we were in the process of the transition, Mykel's wife was excited about all her Scentsy candles. Mykel was very vocal on which ones he could tolerate and which ones he couldn't. Luckily, his wife is very understanding of some of Mykel's issues.

Spiritual Purpose

Animals have wonderful abilities to smell. Jesse tells me the sense of smell also includes smelling the energy flow, rather than the object, as animals do. Humans use this in the same way but have forgotten how to use it. Those humans who spend time in nature have a more refined sense of smell.

Every object, including people, plants, and animals, gives off an energy field. This vibrational energy field can be sensed by smell. Jesse said that food has a good smell when it is fresh due to clear energy, but as it gets older and rots, the energy field is tainted, causing a smell. Openhearted people have higher vibrational energy, which makes them smell better than those closed-off people whose energy is tainted with negativity.

My friend Linda can smell when family members who have passed are around her. She will smell her grandfather's aftershave when her grandfather's spirit is around her.

Jesse does not have a sense of smell, just as one of his eardrums does not move. The medical doctors state this occurred because of the bad spot on his brain stem. Jesse believes it is tied to his inability to have memories. He does not recall much of his childhood or, really, too many days in the past. For us this makes sense: no smell and no memory are both tied to the limbic system. Why did this occur for Jesse? I believe it was part of his soul's choice, to help him focus on the "here and now" rather than being stuck in the past as so many others become trapped. What an interesting concept—the ability to not have the self-doubt or negative thoughts about past mistakes.

ROPE OR STRAP
BOY'S RIGGINS

HALLOWEEN
AND
VACUUMING

MESSY   JESSE

MYKEL ALWAYS SWINGING AND JESSE NOT!!!

JESSE'S CREATIONS   PARK TIME

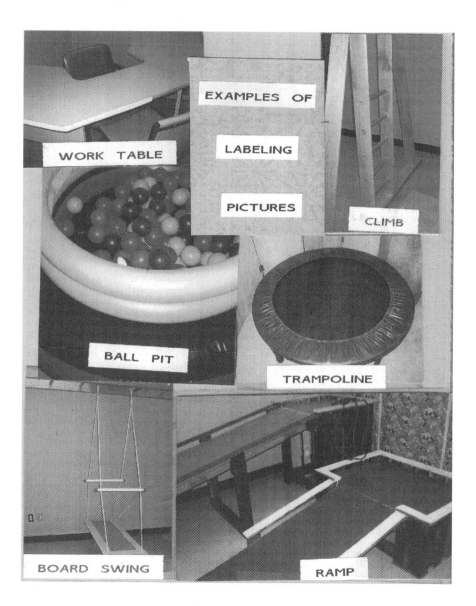

EXAMPLES OF

LABELING

PICTURES

WORK TABLE

CLIMB

BALL PIT

TRAMPOLINE

BOARD SWING

RAMP

CHAPTER 8

PROPRIOCEPTIVE (HIDDEN SENSE): MUSCLES AND JOINTS

Medical Definition

This sense is one of my favorites. Working with young children, you learn quickly how important the proprioceptive sense can be. Children seem to spend their days in constant motion. Our muscles and joints help us with regulation. *Proprioceptive* means "one's own" or individual sense. So it is our own sense of our muscles and joints. This is different from interoception, which is our internal sense of things like tiredness, or exteroception, which is how we perceive the world around us. The receptors in our muscles work with our inner ears to help us move through space.

Key Points:

- Proprioceptive sense uses muscle and joints, along with the nervous system, to communicate how the body moves through space and how much strength is needed for tasks.

- Proprioception (from *proprio*, Latin for "one's own") means we take in sensory information that lets us know our movements or body positions. It helps us integrate touch and movement.
- Receptors for the proprioceptive sense are in the muscles and joints. But ligaments, tendons, and connective tissues also contribute. The stimuli for these receptors are movement and gravity.
- This sense helps your brain know where body parts are, as well as how your body moves through space, without your looking at them.
- It feels how body parts work together.
- It determines muscle movement, timing, and force used in tasks.
- It involves motor planning and control.
- It modulates arousal level
- It is seldom the only impaired system.

Layman's Terms

Proprioception informs us how we move through space. It is the sense that tells us when we have put a foot on a stair step; our body will sense that the foot has stopped and we will no longer force our foot onto the step. Sometimes the information does not register back correctly. A child, when stacking blocks, may try to keep forcing a block onto the next one without getting the idea that the block is already in place.

People who have difficulty in this area are said to have motor-planning issues. These individuals have difficulty moving through space and have trouble with daily movement or completion of tasks. They may be labeled as klutzes.

Children's Behaviors

When I work with parents, I teach them to read the child's behaviors and provide the sensory input he or she needs. For example, children with proprioceptive issues seek lots of muscle and joint input by climbing, jumping, pushing, and pulling. I would call them the "furniture movers." I tell parents to read the behavior. If the child was climbing the back of the couch, a parent would still set a limit and tell the child not to climb the couch. But instead of the natural reaction to have the child sit down, a parent could offer movement activities, such as jumping on a trampoline or climbing on playground equipment.

Both of our children were extremely active. We would plan lots of physical activities all day to help them regulate their bodies. Jesse was in constant motion. Due to his hearing issues, Jesse was drawn to vacuum cleaners. He did not just play with them—Jesse at a very young age knew how to work them. He knew all the parts and knew how to wind the cord; he vacuumed for hours. Yes, I have this on videotape just to prove his obsession with them! We literally went through four Red Dirt Devil vacuums, as Jesse wore them out.

On Halloween, my friend Kathy came over. Mykel had dressed up. Mykel was fearful of the dark and dogs, so he refused to go trick-or-treating even though he was five years old and used to walking the neighborhood with his mom.

He stood on the front porch and gave out candy. Mykel was very social and had great language. He would complement everyone who came up to the door. He would say, "You look amazing, Tinker Bell" or "Wow, you're so scary." We lived on an Air Force base, and on Halloween there were lots of families trick-or-treating for hours. Kathy asked what we were going to do with Jesse, since he was about eighteen months old and didn't attend to anything for any length of time. I pulled out the vacuum cleaner. Jesse played for an hour and a half in the entryway.

Sensory Activities

- pulling and pushing tasks, including wagons, swings, tug of war, etc
- obstacle courses (inside and out), tunnels, boxes, etc
- hanging from monkey bars, using ropes hanging from a ramp or bar that have knots tied at intervals
- activities such as horseback riding or hippotherapy, tumbling, dancing, and sports
- playing horsey, wheelbarrow walking, or—our favorite—having the children help in the garden, including pushing a wheelbarrow
- hammering things while helping with building, ripping paper, crafts
- pillow or snowball fights, playing catch with heavy balls (which you can find in catalogues or with the workout equipment)

Physical activity has always worked as an aid to learning. There have been the scientific studies of how the brain functions and the role of physical activity. One of the things that has stood out for me is the theory of bottom-up learning. Our brain's natural flow comes from the brain stem, through the motor track (neuro pathway) through the attention/regulation area, through our emotions, and finally to the area of language.

When you look at how we communicate with children in schools and at home, you will see that we use the top-down method. We give them commands. We activate the area of language first and expect a response. Many children with regulatory issues cannot respond well to this method. But if we first activate movement, then we will see a more positive response.

For example, a teacher may give verbal instructions in the classroom, but several boys may not be listening. She could have the children who are not focused do physical tasks, such as moving books for her or taking something to the office. Rather than single out the boys, she could have the entire class get up, move to music, march around the room, move outside for the lesson, or just have them do some arm push-ups on their desks. This movement helps the brain flow better and organizes the brain to receive the verbal instruction.

Adult Behaviors

Our boys had lots of physical movement as children. As they got older, the need to have such intense muscle movement faded. They still describe the intensity of focus for video games, etc. but not so much in the physical way. The boys used physical exercise to help with regulation but needed it less and less as they moved into adulthood. Both boys are uncoordinated in their movements. They never were athletes. Mykel described working at the parts store, knocking down boxes as he went down the aisles, and having to go pick things up. We often describe Jesse as a "bull in a china shop." It is interesting to watch them plan their movements through a room.

Spiritual Purpose

Our muscles and joints are the connection to mind, body, and soul. They provide the signals to the brain not only for movement but for our position in space, as well. Those that have spiritual experiences, often describe an "out-of-body" feeling. The soul can vibrate at a higher frequency, giving the body a detached feeling. It is the proprioceptive system that grounds the body and reestablishes the connection. Many people use grounding exercises to help them feel more calm and connected. You may walk barefoot on the grass, touch a tree, sit by a fire, go for a swim, or walk outside. These are not only muscle and joint work; they also help the body find balance in the mind-body-soul connection. The spiritual purpose of our muscles and joints is to help us calm and regulate while grounding our soul to this earthly plane.

Jesse describes this system as "the spirit is the power behind the system. If the spirit leaves (death), then the body goes limp. The spirit powers the nervous system, which allows the muscles and tendons to work. The soul is the engine that pumps the oil throughout the system so that it works. Mind-body-soul is a delicate balance system. If one is off balance, then the others are affected."

CHAPTER 9

VESTIBULAR (HIDDEN SENSE): INNER EAR

Medical Definition

The vestibular system is located in the inner ear. This system helps with balance, muscle tone, and movement. It helps us know where the body is in relationship to other objects. The system helps us with movement and motor planning.

Main Points:

- The vestibular system is located in the inner ear. It sends messages to the part of the brain that controls eye movements, balance/movement, and muscle tone.
- The vestibular system tells us where our heads and bodies are in relation to the ground.
- This system takes in sensory messages about balance and movement from the neck, eyes, and body. It sends these messages to the central nervous system for processing and then helps generate muscle tone that allows the body to move smoothly and efficiently.
- It is the organizer of all sensory input.
- It senses inner ear-movement, gravity, and vibration.

- It helps the body move through space and against gravity.
- It controls muscle tone and posture.
- It guides the body in which direction and how fast to go.
- It develops left-to-right and top-down eye movement for basic reading.
- It controls the level of alertness.
- It stabilizes the visual field as the head and neck move.

Layman's Terms

The vestibular system helps us know how our bodies are moving through space. It helps us to keep our heads upright. If you have ever had a bad inner ear infection, you will understand how difficult it is to keep your head upright when your balance is off. Those that crave vestibular input love roller coasters, swinging, or hanging upside down. Those with vestibular insecurity do not like getting off the ground. They hate roller coasters. They may get carsick. Jesse has lots of issues with vestibular insecurity. He did not learn to swing until he was eight years of age. He never learned to ride a bike. This affects his driving abilities, as he has problems with planning and depth perception. I believe that many children who do not learn to ride a bike are affected by this, and it will cause driving difficulties later on. We will discuss this in detail in the adult section.

Children's Behaviors

When Mykel was born, our parents lived two hours away in different directions. Both sets of parents wanted us to come see them at least monthly. Initially, we tried to visit as often as we could, but Mykel could not tolerate riding in the car. He never fell asleep. He would scream nonstop for the entire two hours unless we stopped the car. We would pull over to let him calm down and then try driving again. We never let our kids out of car seats, so that was not his issue. It wasn't until later that I learned of his vestibular issues. We stopped traveling for several years due to his crying. We just could not tolerate it.

Sensory Activities

- turning circles or spinning like a top
- swings—our center had many swings: Lycra-type hammocks, board swings, swings that are chair/hammock shaped
- merry-go-round, seesaws, teeter-totters, balance beam, walking curb or low wall
- trampoline or mattress (especially waterbed mattresses that can be filled with air or water)
- stairs, slides, hills to roll down, ramps, or scooters
- running in circles, walking on uneven surfaces (which is the best way to treat vestibular insecurities)
- flips in a pool, water slides, wave pools

Adult Behaviors

Mykel and Jesse today say that they tend to fall over easily. They will stand up to walk, get dizzy, and catch themselves. Jesse never learned to ride his bike, which affects his spatial awareness now that he is learning to drive (still working on it for two years now). All these are issues with his vestibular insecurity.

Mykel loves the movement and speed of the roller coaster. On his first time to Disney World, Mykel began thinking that whoever was in front of the roller coaster was driving, but he had not shared this. When we went to Space Mountain, I was in front. When we got off, Mykel stated, "Mama, you drive fast." He still loves that thrill today, and it shows in his fast driving. Jesse, on the other hand, isn't comfortable driving over forty-five miles per hour.

In fact, Jesse lost his fast-speed button when he had heart issues as a child. He went from a blur running by to a very slow-moving child. When you say, "Jesse, you will be late for class! You need to hurry," there is not a difference in the way he walks—unless it is even slower. Jesse states he just does not like to move fast, because he cannot process what is happening when he goes too fast. He said this is the difficulty with driving. He wants to concentrate on one thing at a time, and there are multiple things to do when you are driving.

Spiritual Purpose

Vestibular sense is the sense of being present in the moment. Without being present in the moment you would not know what was around you. Those who crave the vestibular input force must be fully attentive and present in the moment. This helps increase body awareness, which increases the connection with mind-body-soul. Martial-arts sparring also uses movement and muscles to increase the present-in-the-moment connection.

Those who avoid vestibular input also avoid being present in the moment. They either want to be in the past, reliving good memories, or in the future, where they see the light. When Jesse was a young child, he did not want to be present on this earth. He often talked about leaving and told us how he missed God. He spent lots of his time talking with spirits rather than being present in the moment. Jesse states that the drawback to not being present in the moment is that it opens you up to other things controlling you.

CHAPTER 10

INTEROCEPTION (INTERNAL SENSE: SENSING ENERGY) AND EXTEROCEPTION (SENSING STIMULUS OUTSIDE OF THE BODY)

Medical Definition

Interoception means sensitivity to input coming from inside of the body. This sense is responsible for detecting internal states. This provides awareness of an individual's overall body state, such as tiredness or tension. This also provides input on emotional states such as anger, happiness, etc.

Exteroception means sensing input outside of the body. People take in sensory information from the environment. Sometimes animals take in sensory input more than humans do. Certain animals have heightened senses in order to survive. Some are able to sense electrical and magnetic fields, and others can detect water pressure and currents. Some humans have the abilities to perceive the energy of the environment, presence of things unseen, and intent of others.

Layman's Terms

Many therapists use the *How Does Your Engine Run?* book and program by Williams and Shellenberger to teach children and adults modulation of their own systems. We used this with our boys to teach them to feel whether their engines were revving or slowing down (Williams and Shellenberger, 1996).

Children's Behaviors

Children's behaviors are driven by a need that must be met. Children have difficulty interpreting their internal states and verbally expressing their emotions. They can become easily overwhelmed by external stimuli, including noisy places, overloading lights, and too much visual stimulation. Many times as parents when a child becomes overwhelmed or upset, we tend to say "You're ok". We negate how children are feeling and limit the chance for children to identify their own feelings or body states. As parents, we can help children identify these by stating what is happening. For example, "I see that you are tired and getting upset." Or "You are anger that brother took your toy". Many times we only have to acknowledge or reflect back the feeling or body state to help children find their own way instead of solving problems for them.

Sensory Activities

- Help children learn to recognize their own body state, using comparisons like the "car revving up or slowing down."
- Learn to limit overstimulation by lights, television, etc.
- Learn activities that help calm and organize the body.
- Reflect or restate a child's internal state or feeling.
- Help children learn to identify and express feelings in appropriate ways.

Adult Behaviors

Both boys are easily overwhelmed by external environments like Wal-Mart or being in crowds. Mykel describes having difficulty managing himself at work with several people around him behind the counter area. Jesse has issues at school. He describes being susceptible to others' energy; this disrupts his ability to manage his own energy. He describes those people who tend to drain his energy and then leave him to manage his own lack of internal organization. Mykel avoids crowds and being in front of people at all cost. Jesse chooses to go into theater to learn to deal with being in front a crowd of people.

Spiritual Purpose

The spirit also plays a part in how individuals perceive input. Examples of this are people with high tolerance of pain or those that are very sensitive. The soul, or spirit, is the connection to God. This connection is the eternal link with God. When a person learns to quiet his mind through prayer, meditation, mindfulness practices, or other strategies, the soul is the "present-in-the-moment" feeling. The soul helps to quiet the mind's constant chatter and therefore creates awareness of the internal body states and external stimuli. The soul's natural state is silence and the in-the-moment feeling. If you come from the soul, then you are always in the moment and peaceful. The moment in time can be felt and can resonant at a higher vibrational frequency.

This moment occurs, of course, in occasions such as weddings, births of children, deaths, etc. In those moments, we realize the importance of our existence and the preciousness of the here and now. In essence, our constant chatter in our minds is the *ego*, which seeks to keep us separate from God through negative thoughts. The *soul* is the connection with God that is cleared or strengthened through calming the mind and practicing being present in the moment.

We teach these moments in trauma work, to help others stop flashback symptoms by focusing on the body's reactions (the feel of their arms or legs) and the environmental sensory input (sights, sounds, smells, etc.). This orients the person to the present moment. More importantly, we learn that the past has already left and the future does not exist. The present moment is all that there is.

CHAPTER 11

EMOTIONS (HEART SENSE)

Medical Definition

When we began writing this book, I was explaining to my boys the different sensory systems that I have described above. Jesse informed me there is another sense, called the *heart sense*. I had not heard of this. I included the topic title but had no information on it. One weekend when I was concentrating on writing this book, I came to this section. I told Jesse that I would need his help that day, since this was his idea and I had no information on it. He laughed and said okay.

Shortly after this, I had a friend call whom I had not spoken to for a long time. She was sharing her life and some health issues with me. I was explaining the emotional connection to the mind of the physical body and spoke of the book *You Can Heal Your Life,* by Louise Hay. I was talking to her and going to Louise Hay's website when I stumbled across the following website: www.enlightenedfeelings.com, by Lori D'Ascenzo.

Lori D'Ascenzo had the "seventh sense—the heart." I started to laugh so hard. Spirit always gives the message right on time. When we do not rush, push, or try to control our lives, spirit will guide us. Over the next few days, God provided many references, including the HeartMath project at www.heartmath.org. Here is my understanding of the heart sense; if this resonates with you, then investigate these wonderful sites.

I have always believed that our thoughts create our lives and state of health. Most people believe that you have a bodily pain and then you think about the pain. I believe instead that our thoughts are *creating* the body's response. I learned that the heart may be sending the response to the mind through the heartbeat! So our emotions and hearts may be telling our brains, which send the signals to our bodies. All animals and humans have an emotional sense that some refer to as a "heart" sense. This sense helps them to understand what might be helpful or harmful to them and whether or not their needs are being met.

In attachment theory, I had learned that emotions come from either love (positive emotions) or fear (negative emotions). Love includes emotions such as happiness, contentment, and joy. Fear-based emotions include anger, hurt, and resentment. When children are infants, they experience discomfort (hunger, thirst, being wet, etc.) and then they cry. The parent responds, and the need is met. The children learn to trust that their feelings and needs are being met. This leads them to form attachment to others. This begins the development of empathy and caring for others. This helps develop the heart sense.

As a counselor, I have spent many years teaching young children and their families that all emotions are okay, even the negative ones. Our society tends to teach people not to express their emotions, especially the negative or fear-based ones. Animals trust their intuitions; this keeps them alive. Humans tend to dismiss emotions or try to rationalize them. Emotions help tell us what is going on internally. They can protect us and give a sense of well-being. Negative emotions are intense, but they help us to take action and lead to change. Anger can fuel righting a wrong or changing society, like, for example, the organization MADD, Mothers Against Drunk Driving. When we are in fear, our stress cycle gets kicked on to protect us from danger.

When children get their needs met, they form connections to others. They learn that connections help them meet their needs and desires. We are each responsible for getting our own needs met. When we do not get our needs met, then negative emotions can begin, including loneliness, resentment, hurt, guilt, shame, and anger. When the negative emotions begin, then self-doubt and self-esteem issues may arise. Frustration can occur when we cannot effectively get our needs met, even as young children. Depression is the process of closing the heart sense down. This deeply affects the mind and body.

I have taught many foster parents about the needs behind a child's behavior. I have taught others to acknowledge feelings, help children learn to identify those feelings, and accept the messages the feelings are sending. Feelings are not wrong; they are your messengers. We must acknowledge the feeling and then decide on the response. Respond instead of reacting. Decide your actions from your awareness, not from hiding those feelings.

Layman's Terms

Children are born with open hearts and very sensitive needs. How do we help them in a world that focuses on the pain? The word *conscious* means to "know well." In today's fast-paced world, with nonstop reports of violence and heartache, how can our heart sense understand and know how to respond to this information? The study for mind-and-body relationship began more than thirty years ago in Russia, when scientists discovered neuropeptides. The neuropeptides signal molecules that influence the brain. Thus they affect many brain functions, including social behaviors, reproduction, learning, and memory, as well as metabolism, food intake, etc. The study of neuropeptides helped start our understanding of how our emotions affect our health. When we talked about the stress cycle before, we discussed how stress or some emotional responses trigger the release of adrenalin and cortisol. Cortisol has become one of the most researched chemicals recently. Emotional balance releases endorphins which help our overall health.

Many research universities are now studying the connection with emotions and the body. One of the studies focuses on how emotions affect the immune system. Louise Hay who wrote *You Can Heal Your Life and Heal your body* has written and taught about this connection for many years. Each emotion has its own frequency of vibration which helps the body to release certain neuropeptides in the body.

The Fear based emotions have a lower frequency range, while Love emotions have higher frequencies. Unconditional love of course has the highest frequency wavelength. You can see this change if you have ever seen someone who was very angry and something funny happens. The angry person begins to laugh. The change in frequencies releases different neuropeptides. This helps balance or nullifies the negative emotion.

Children's Behaviors

When working with parents, I often talk about learning to read their children's behaviors. With the sensory system, the child's brain will crave input they need, until they get it. For example, they will climb when the need Proprioceptive input, hang upside down on a couch or chair when they need Vestibular input. I try to get parents to recognize the behaviors as the sign for what the child is needing. The same is said for the Heart sense. We must help children learn to recognize emotions and a way of expressing them that is not harmful to themselves or others. When Jesse had a hard time regulating anger emotions, we would get him to laugh. This would change his hormones, produce more endorphins, and increase his frequency resulting in the reduction of anger.

Sensory Activities

- Learn to identify feelings (feeling charts or videos).
- Trust a child's first thoughts or feelings or intuition.
- Don't force a child to interact with someone they are not comfortable around.

Adult Behaviors

Jesse was describing at baccalaureate a woman who came up and said the longest prayer he ever heard. During the prayer, he said he did not hear her words but the emotion coming off her. He could feel her strong emotion. As I explained earlier, Mykel could always sense the emotions in a room. Even as an adult, he describes sensing others' intent or emotions. This is overwhelming for Mykel, so he withdraws, often into video games, or sitting around the fire pit, or leaving the area.

Spiritual Purpose

The heart is like a compass; it guides you on the path you have chosen. Humans are the only mammals that override the heart sense of danger. I have worked with women who were battered and abused as kids. They frequently override the sense of danger with thoughts from the ego. They say things like "He promised to be better," or "My mom needed me," and often place themselves in more danger. The ego talks the person into overriding the heart sense (gut feeling). Trusting the heart sense is learned by practice. Jesse stated if you can listen to your heart, you can tell which life path is helpful. Trust your intuition—heart sense, gut feeling—it is there to protect you."

The HeartMath research is an incredible project by Doc Childre. These researchers call the heart sense a "heart intuitive intelligence." They maintain that the heart can send information to the brain by an energetic system. They have found that the heart sends information to the brain through the heartbeat. Emotions affect the heartbeat. The heart generates a magnetic field around the body that can be felt, through physiological response, by others. When the body comes to a coherent state between the heart and brain, then creative solutions and intuition are at their best. But when choices are made by ego, they override intuition.

The intuitive heart is the access point for our own internal wisdom. This energetic field drives our biological systems, which drives our behaviors, choices, and results. Human emotions are connected to this field. Research on prefeelings found that the heart sense responded three to five seconds before some stimulus. Individuals were shown pictures that made them feel neutral or calm and ones that stirred an emotional response. Individuals responded by heart changes before seeing the emotional picture. (*Electrophysiological Evidence of Intuition: Part 1. The Surprising Role of the Heart*, and *Part 2. A System-Wide Process?*) A study called *Predictive Physiological Anticipation Preceding Seemingly Unpredictable Stimuli* showed that the brain picks up what is about to happen in an energetic (marked by energy) way. The brain can perceive it three to five seconds before it happens. See http://www.frontiersin.org/perception_science.

Jesse stated that the "heart senses the intention of the movement before the action occurs." We are all connected and are all one. When we look at quantum entanglements, we see that, after being separated, cells that were together still respond together. Dr. Glen Rein did research on love sent with conscious intent transforming the DNA molecule and healing it with loving energy. He found that specific thoughts/intentions from the mind can modulate with the frequency of the bio field of the heart. When we are in love, the coherence of the bio fields grows stronger. Resonance occurs between the coherence of the heart and the coherence fields around DNA molecules. The intent causes change in the DNA. See http://www.item-bioenergy.com/infocenter. As we speak, feel, think, and respond, we are affecting each other. You can choose how you will respond. Will you be the one to respond with empathy, compassion, or love?

CHAPTER 12

AUTISM

Medical Definition

Autism is currently considered a neurological disorder that affects language and social development with stereotypical behaviors. Most of the stereotypical behaviors are sensory in nature. The *autism spectrum* includes those diagnosed on one end with pervasive developmental disorder, through autism, to Asperger syndrome on the other end.

Layman's Terms

I have spent most of my counseling career working with children who have autism or special needs. I have always considered this to be an honor to me, and not only because of any help that I may give them. If you have a family member with autism, then you know how incredible these children are to the world. Many people have wondered: why are so many children diagnosed with autism? What is their true purpose on earth? Let's start by looking at some basic information about how autistic children process the world.

All children with autism have sensory integration issues. These are the behaviors most people think of, such as hand-flapping, limiting touch, poor eye contact, etc. The difference with children with severe sensory issues and children with autism is in the ability to communicate their needs and use social relationships. Children with autism have difficulty understanding that in order to get their needs met they must connect with others. These children will go to the refrigerator and scream instead of asking for food. They will take someone's hand and put it on the object wanted instead of pointing or asking for the object.

Their language may begin at a normal age but typically stops around fifteen to eighteen months of age. Many do not regain language until three to five years of age. When they do begin to speak, the language is different. Most children learn language beginning with one-word utterances, then two words, etc. Children with autism learn in phrases and exactly the way they hear the phrases.

One of my clients through the Early Intervention Program was a thirteen-month old named Nicole. She was brought into the program for her gross-motor delays. She would scoot around backward on her bottom, instead of walking. The physical therapist had only been in the home a few times when she came to me and asked for a consult. I was brought in due to Nicole's lack of language, limited eye contact, intolerance to touch, and unusual play behaviors. Not only did I work with the family, but over the years we became friends, and her family has allowed me to share her story with so many others. My friend Nicole learned language through Disney movies. She would speak phrases from the movies when something in the environment triggered a memory. One day her mother was brushing her hair as she sat looking into a mirror. This triggered a memory from the movie *Little Mermaid*. Nicole muttered, "Oh, why bother?" Many people were impressed by her great manners. Her mother would say, "Well, it's because of Disney movies."

My friend Kathy has a grandson who is autistic. Kathy had a dog named Molly. Molly loved to bark to welcome the grandson every time he visited. Kathy was always saying, "Shut up, Molly." What Kathy's grandson learned was the name for dogs was "Shut up, Molly." Whenever he saw a dog, he would say, "Shut up, Molly."

Initially Kathy's grandson didn't play with toys appropriately. Rather, he would open and close cabinet doors and drawers, never removing anything from them, just obsessively opening and closing the doors and drawers. When he became upset at home, he would kick and damage the bedroom doors. Once when Kathy's grandson was at her home, he became upset and kicked the playroom door. After getting into trouble for kicking the door, every time he walked down the hall past the playroom he would say, "Don't kick a door."

Since sensory integration is a primary issue with autistic children, helping them regulate their bodies is important. These children may need lots of sensory activities. Some children benefit from textural play, several baths in a day, or the wearing of headphones to limit input. I recommend that children with autism complete the brushing program to help them with tolerating the environment. I encourage parents to release their old ideas of parenting. The focus should be on helping the child to self-regulate. For my friend Nicole, that meant multiple baths a day. Her family learned to accept this need in order to make the day more tolerable.

Autistic children are visual learners. The cones and rods in their eyes are shaped differently so that they see in more pixels. This causes poor vision in the center of their eyes, so they see better from the side (peripheral). They also tend to line things up or prefer to walk fence lines due to this difference in their vision.

They also receive all sensory information at once and at the same level. So when they walk into a room, they take in all the sensory information. They will hear a ceiling fan moving, light flickering, or the refrigerator humming at the same level as someone talking to them. This can be extremely overwhelming and can lead to behavioral outbursts.

Visual learners use nonverbal, or visual, cues. Their auditory systems are faulty. Although hearing may be normal, the neural pathways are as busy as a traffic jam. The auditory information does not process well. Auditory commands should be limited or not used at all. Classroom routine and organization should be centered on visual cues. Using visual cues with your words will increase the children's understanding of what you need them to do.

When working with these visual learners, we label all items in their environment. We use label makers or write the names of objects on that objects. This also helps in reading. We use color-coded to help visually link objects. For example we would give the same color folders to match the textbooks. A green science book would go with the green folder. We place things in the left folder pocket for "Work" side and then the child places it in the right folder pocket for "Finished". This helps pattern the brain for reading (tracking left to right).

Teaching should depend on visual aids or demonstrations and limit auditory instruction.

We begin with simple sorting or matching—the beginning step for most children—and we teach this in either a Structured Teaching method or Applied Behavior Analysis (ABA). This means we increase the difficulty of the task, but one change at a time; we break down tasks into steps. Matching begins with the object itself (concrete object) and moves to more abstract (actual picture, then drawing, then line drawing or symbol). We do repetitive exercises to help with attention, focus, and learning. We focus on what objects are and the purpose of objects.

Advanced sorting includes learning letters, numbers, and sight-reading words and examining the same and different; it enhances language by giving a verbal clue along with the visual object. Children with autism have issues with social relationships. Their brain functions like a computer with exceptional memory. They record events like a DVD or videotape. Every detail is etched into their brains, just like a computer hard drive. They do not easily understand the function of relationship systems. This causes issues in learning and social development.

It is hard for them to use gestures to have their needs met, since most gestures include some social contact or context. Gestures require joint attention—both people must share attention to the same object. This can be encouraged by touching the object instead of pointing to it from a distance, for example, reading books and touching the pictures, touching the object the child might be requesting, etc.

Don't assume the child understands the words you are saying. She or he may be responding to your tone of voice or to only a few of the words. Although the child may be able to say lots of words, this does not mean her understanding of the words exists. She or he may have memorized the words without the meaning or correct use.

Imitation can be taught, starting with simple action of a toy or task. A more difficult skill is imitation of action that cannot be seen, like working a puppet where the hand is not visible. Imitation of complex steps or difficult motor tasks can be challenging. Often children with sensory issues also have poor motor planning.

Imitation, cause and effect, and role play are very challenging to children with autism. These are natural ways of learning with other children, but they are difficult for someone with autism, because they require a social contact. We started services with Nicole at a very young age, because she had motor delays. She also did not like to be held and never made eye contact. One day, when the room was full of her parents, grandparents and early intervention people, this little girl knocked over her sippy cup and the adults all said, "Uh-oh." She paused and then picked it up, and all the adults went "Yay!" and clapped. So she knocked it over again. We did this for twenty minutes, because we wanted her to get cause and effect.

Children's Behaviors

The first games infants play are face-to-face games, like peek-a-boo. Social games are very difficult; they require interaction and imitation. Typical development begins with social skills, moves to playing with toys, and then evolves to motor skills. Children with autism seem to develop this in reverse, since their motor skills are stronger, and playing with objects comes later. Pretend play is difficult, since this requires imitation of adult behaviors and social interaction.

We sometimes teach the children how to look more appropriate, since children with autism see no point to pretend play. We worked on the steps of pretend play, how to imitate others, and that the purpose of play was to have friends. Cause-and-effect concepts influence how we work with objects. Children with autism may not understand a toy's purpose—for example, that a car is for rolling along a road, not for flipping over and spinning the wheels. They have issues with following a sequence, for example, driving a car down the road to the gas station—and then what?

After children get the concept of how the toy is used, we change the play to vary the routine, and we add another step. We put different kinds of toys together, like a doll that goes in the car for a ride. This same concept for teaching can be used for mastering routines or sequences of events—beginning with the basic and adding steps, one at a time. It is important to not miss a step. We must teach the task exactly as we want them to learn it, since they remember it exactly as taught.

Children may have issues tolerating peers. We need to introduce peers gradually. Be in the same room, and expect the child with autism to need more time. Do activities at the same table but still not together. Share materials for the project with other children. Have the child get closer to the group with an older child as a mentor. Then, slowly include the child in the group activities.

Children as mentors can help teach social skills, especially through games. The mentor may need to explain why the child with autism does not understand all the social rules and how other children can help.

Facts—concrete items—are easily memorized. Autistic children have a videotape on and recording. They have extremely good memories for details. They do well in school for subjects like history or math, which do not involve a lot of social cues. They may struggle with subjects that change often or require social context.

When you teach skills, be careful that they are taught in the proper way and at the proper times. Autistic children will not vary from the routine. I remember a child who was taught by his therapist and teacher to undress and dress. This was done when the children went to lunch. The child would go behind a screen and practiced dressing. What he really learned was that before lunch you take your clothes off and then put them back on.

When Kathy's grandson first experienced going to the movies with Grammy, she took him when very few people were attending. He became fascinated with the rows of seats and the lights on each side of the aisle. He started out standing next to Grammy at the end of the aisle and then began to move forward and move up and down the aisle. Although he wasn't bothering anybody at the time, it was important to stop the behavior, or he would have thought it was always okay to walk up and down the aisle during the movie. He had to learn appropriate behavior at appropriate times.

Children with autism may be able to recite names or use concepts, but they cannot comprehend the meaning. My friend, whom I spoke of earlier, learned about condensation in school. Nicole memorized the information and passed her test with As. A year later, her mother was taking her to school one morning, this little girl saw the condensation on the car window. She asked her mother what it was, and for the first time, she understood the concept.

Key Points:

- poor impulse control
- likes routine and structure
- easily distracted
- easily overwhelmed by sensory input or environment
- faulty auditory system
- poor cause and effect
- focus on non-important details (lights, sensory input, noises, etc.)
- compulsiveness and cognitive rigidity (don't change the routine)
- poor body regulation/movement
- limited social skills and/or play skills
- poor use of language to get needs met

When we are working with clients in the school setting, we want to focus on helping children manage themselves throughout the day. The academic part of school will not typically be the issue. The problems arise in regulation of an active environment that is unpredictable and involves lots of social interaction.

Suggestions for Inclusion at School

- Clearly defined goals and well-written IEP (Individualized Educational Plan) with outlined responsibilities. This is a true team approach. The focus must remain on what is best for the child's regulation in the classroom.
- Defined modifications across all areas to ensure consistency (coach, counselors, bus drivers, teachers, lunch room).
- Work on critical skills such as regulation, working quietly, completing tasks, working independently, and communicating (how to get needs met) to reduce behavioral issues.
- Waiting supports (can be sensory in nature, fidgets, something to bite on, sand play, etc.) help children manage over stimulating environments.
- Spatial awareness avoids sensory overloads (may need to leave classroom before the bell rings to avoid the noise and movement of the other students).
- Calendars/schedules/charts consistent at school, home, and with other caregivers are excellent visual tools.
- Labeled areas for materials, color-coded books and folders, etc. help with organization and consistency.

- Predictable routines, with visual aids for the routine or any changes can reduce behavioral outburst.
- Use of calendars allow the child to understand what will happen next. (Start with poster board on the wall at home, with pictures of family, places they go, favorite things, and routines, like going in the bathtub. Then laminate them. Use Velcro dots on the back of the pictures and poster board. Use them to show the child the daily routine. You can show him the picture is changing if the routine changes. As he grows older, include visual calendars at school and transition to agendas and electronic calendars.)
- Choice boards (choice between certain options) help children feel that they have some since of control in their lives and reduces fighting.
- Highlighting important information offers visual tracking to the key items.
- Verbal instructions offered with visual cues help memory retention.
- Planned stress reduction breaks help the brain work better at attending when school work resumes. (Include sensory, such as movement, muscle work, tactile play, or snack.)

Visual Instructions

It is very important to follow this consistently. I stress this to all my parents and teachers. This is not only wonderful for children with autism but all children in the classroom. For all children can benefit from clear consistent instructions.

- What do I need to do?
- Where do I begin?
- What order?
- What does "finished" look like? (All the work in the blue folder on the left side is work to be done, and work that is finished is moved to the right side.)
- What do I do next?

Stress Reduction Breaks

- Have a cool-down period before things escalate. Hopefully have set aside a "calm place."
- Provide heavy work—movement—and limit environmental inputs (lights, noise). Have the child help the teachers move books. Have all the children stretch, due push-ups against the wall, march around the room, etc.
- Organize tactile play.
- Limit verbal instructions or add a visual cue.
- If the adults or other children are stressed/excited, then calming their responses can sometimes help the child with autism manage the environment. Sometimes all it takes is turning off the lights or background noises to help calm the environment. (http://teacch.com)

If I can only convey one thing to school personnel, I hope this will be the most important thing. Children who are dysregulated need movement and heavy work to calm down. This is best done on the playground. Whether it is a child with ADHD, autism, or anything in between, *please do not take away recess as a behavioral consequence.* It is the running on the playground that helps children focus in school.

Adult Behaviors

My friend Nicole is now in college. Many families believe that their young child will not achieve independence. Adults with autism are still very routine-oriented and still rely on visual cues. They usually find jobs that are very specific, such as military services or jobs that involve detailed paperwork or rote tasks. They are usually very knowledgeable and can learn elaborate systems. In Chapel Hill, South Carolina, there is a center that works with individuals with autism. The form of instruction they use is called Structured Teaching (TEACCH). There is an elaborate bus system in the town, but the individuals with autism know the bus system better than anyone else. Their strengths are in incredible memory and attention to details.

Spiritual Purpose

One of the important aspects of raising children with autism is helping them feel good about their strengths. Kathy's grandson is old enough to know that he memorizes information easily. He was discussing this issue with his "Grammy." Kathy told him that it was a gift. She was encouraging him by saying, "If you wanted to be a doctor, you could learn this by reading books." Kathy's grandson replied, "But I may have to read them twice."

Jesse related to me that certain spirits are "archivers." They are here to catalogue knowledge by absorbing and integrating it. "It's like a computer that had a data bank. The computer would go out collect information and return it to the data bank. The purpose is to retrieve the information, and social aspects are not the priority. Their brain[s] can hold a huge amount of knowledge." If you have ever been around a person with autism, you will know that knowledge is very important. My friend Nicole would memorize zoo cards with endless information about animals. She would watch TV with other languages in close captioning and memorize French, Spanish, etc. Kathy's grandson loves anything he can read. He memorizes all his Pokemon cards. He knows all the details of each character. Knowledge and information are the purpose for these archive experts. This information is added to the collective consciousness/universal wisdom.

CHAPTER 13

WHAT IS TO COME (SPIRITUAL CHILDREN)

Spiritual Connection

Sensitive people have been recorded in our history through major religions as prophets, medicine people, or shamans. Shamans today still take people on spiritual journeys, through sweat lodges or healings. There are recorded wise men throughout human existence. Today, you can find Morgan Freeman on *Through the Wormhole* discussing research on these subjects. The TV series studies different phenomenon, including the "sixth sense" or ESP. There is research recording our ability to know when someone is watching us without seeing the other person. There are random generators of numbers throughout the world that seem not to be random when global events happen, as, for example, several hours before the 9/11 bombings in New York City. How can we know these events before they occur? We are all connected, and that connection is sometimes called the "collective consciousness" or "collective wisdom." There are sensitive people who can sense that information. See http://noosphere. princeton.edu/papers/ (nelsonpp.pdf)

The Long Island Medium (psychic Theresa Caputo) has been on the *Dr. Oz Show*, where they tried to map her brain during readings. They could show the difference in her brain as she began communicating with those that have transitioned to the other side. Even the *Ghost Hunters* show recorded the energy flow between a medium and the show's host. These are television's versions, but researchers are working on the "proof of God" or explanations for spiritual gifts. This is occurring now before we transition to our next stage of development. We will be able to use our connection with God in a way most can only imagine. This shift has already begun, and we see it with the different types of children being born. We as a society need to look at the purpose of these children and at how we are teaching and rearing them. The old methods are not effective and at times can be harmful to their gifts. Why are these special children here today?

David and I asked ourselves why we had children who were different from others. We needed to know how to help Jesse, with his gifts, and Mykel, with his sensitivity. When my children were young, there were not good answers out in the general public. There were no books from Marianne Williamson or Doreen Virtue or Oprah *Super Soul Sunday*s. One of my favorite books is *Indigo, Crystal, and Rainbow Children*, by Doreen Virtue. This is my understanding of Doreen Virtue's work. How I wish I had had this when my children were younger.

Per Doreen Virtue, "Lightworkers were in answer to prayers during WWII and were born starting in the '50s." Lightworkers were simply to bring light to the world. I was born in the '60s and believe that I am a lightworker. My purpose on this earth is to shine God's light. Lightworkers came at a time when the energy of the world was full of fear and guilt. Just think back to air raids, bomb shelters, and war. So lightworkers learned the ability of disassociation and numbing their feelings. I can tell you, being an abused child, I know how to disassociate and stuff feelings down. When we disagree with someone, we tend to override our own intuition and go along with what we know is not right.

I was a teenager when I began to have dreams that came true. I would have a dream, describe it to my mom, and within a few days it would occur. This caused anxiety in my parents, who held strict religious beliefs that did not accept these occurrences. Looking back, I see that I have always had the gift of wisdom. The light that I emanate is the reason others come to me for questions or tell me their problems. Now I see it as a natural occurrence. Children and animals are very attracted to my presence, as well. My spiritual gifts were dreams that were prophetic or came true.

During these teen years, I had a dream about standing outside of a hospital, although I knew I was not in the hospital. My mom was picking me up in a tan station wagon and was hit by another car at the corner of Sixth and Monroe. My mom dismissed this, since we no longer had a tan station wagon. (For those young people, this is a car that is a cross between a van and a car.)

As a child, I went through physical abuse from my biological father and sexual abuse from both males and females. Much of this I never reported, and as a teen I became suicidal trying to deal with the pain. My stepdad, whom I loved very much, had heart issues. At this time he was going in for surgery. The night before his surgery, I tried to take a bottle of pills. Now, I could have taken a bottle of his heart medication, but we were so trained not to touch his medication that I never thought of it. The only thing we had was Midol. (For the young ones, that is medication for cramps.) I know—stop laughing! Midol did not hurt me, but I did lie there all night with my heart pounding. Needless to say, I cannot take this medication now. The next morning, I asked my mom if I could go with her to the hospital. She said, "Yes, because you look like shit." After my stepdad's surgery, the sleepless night had gotten the better of me. My mom said to call my grandmother and have her pick me up. I was standing outside of the hospital when I heard about the accident. My grandmother had a tan station wagon, and the accident happened on Sixth and Monroe, as she was coming to pick me up. My mom walked out, white and pale. She started to speak, and I said, "I already know." My grandmother was physically okay but emotionally traumatized. My grandmother never drove again, and the guilt was hard to handle. I shut down my ability, due to the pain around me. Lightworkers, or *sensitives*, from my age group tend to override their own gifts in order not to hurt others.

As we briefly discussed what we have learned from Doreen Virtue's description of individuals, Jesse stated that he cannot stand labels of any kind. Jesse sees the soul as it truly is. He wants us all to know how incredible we are. I know that it is difficult to help people understand types of behaviors without some descriptive words. We would like you to concentrate on the descriptions, not the labels.

Indigo (Doreen Virtue)

Indigo children were being born from the 1970s through the early 1990s. These children were born to help move us forward. They have the following traits:

"May become allergic/sensitive to foods and the environment, feel at a deep level, have a good BS detector, are visual learners, and have anger at the state of world/environment/injustice."

They get labeled with attention issues, which she calls "ADHD—Attention Dialed into Higher Dimension."

My Mykel was the child we learned so much from. If I have any regrets in life, it is that I didn't have this information when he was younger. We knew we wanted to parent Mykel differently than the way we had been raised, but it still was not what this sensitive child needed. We changed many things, the first thing being that we would not spank our children. We could see this harmed Mykel's spirit. We used parenting techniques that I had been taught, including Effective Parenting, Love and Logic, etc. We tried to acknowledge Mykel's feelings and encourage his artistic expression. I still feel that we were not on our A game with him.

Maya Angelou says, "When you know better, you do better." I can honestly say I learned as I lived with Mykel. Mykel was everything that was described above. He was very sensitive to things as a child. He had severe allergies and asthma. He was sensory defensive to all touch, sounds, smells, etc. He did have, and continues to have, trouble with sleeping. Mykel always has his BS detector on. He would work with people if he could respect them; he was not impressed with their titles or positions of authority. (Imagine how that worked out in a school setting). While I, as a lightworker, would override my feelings or intuition for other's rules, Mykel would not. He was more likely to push through and do what he thought needed to be done. He was very active and a visual-to-movement learner. He needed to see and feel things. Of course, with attention issues, Mykel would start things but have trouble finishing them.

When the boys were younger, there were many sleep issues, and Mykel never slept alone until his preteen years. We had to keep the boys' rooms more neutral, without over stimulating colors. We had to do prayers at night and ask Archangel Michael to watch over them. Of course little Mykel loved this. My boys hated any dolls looking at them, or mirrors in their rooms, and still do to this day. The emotional expression was our greatest challenge. Mykel had so many outbursts. His anger was our greatest issue. Mykel would be the first to help others, defend the weak, and drag home those in need. We were not able to deal very effectively with his anger toward injustice. In fact, we made many mistakes, mostly in trying to control the expression. This turned him inward more, and he began a brief period of drug use. Looking back now, I would have helped him understand his gifts more and encouraged him to find a spiritual connection that worked with his strengths.

As he is transitioning into adulthood now, I see glimpses of his gifts. He is opening back up and beginning to connect back with spirit. God is more important in his life now. Mykel has always hated medication and is looking more into natural healing methods, which of course was part of his original path. What we learned was that parenting these children is about providing the environment for growth and the knowledge they need. The children already know their true paths and do not respond to any parenting that attempts to control or shape their paths. Parenting for these children has to do with paying attention to the need underneath the behavior, not forcing the behavior to change. It is about helping them manage in a world that is not in sync with them as of yet. But it will change, and they will be our guides.

Crystal (Doreen Virtue)

The first group of *crystal children* was born from the 1990s through the current time. They have gifts fitted for the next change. They have the following characteristics:

"Large eyes look right into you to the depth of your soul; pure love, more sensitive of chemicals/food and can be self-select vegetarians, psychic abilities, speak late due to telepathic abilities, and they have inner radar detectors and look for open hearts."

Jesse does not like labels, as mentioned earlier. He does not want any label to be put on children. He wants children and adults to be seen as the beautiful souls that we are. He wants us all to know how connected we are to God and how powerful we are. Jesse was my sweet angel baby. He was a joy to raise. He had ringlet curls and did not speak until he was three or four years of age, but he did make his needs known. I knew he was communicating with me even though it was not verbally or with gestures. He always got his point across. I would walk away thinking he was one very smart baby.

He was labeled for his shyness. Looking back, I understand more of this behavior. He would literally hide behind me if people tried to talk to him, except for a few people whom he would never be shy around. Now I understand that he was interacting only with those who had open hearts. Even as a young child he would sense adults and children who he did not trust. He was loving and even today gives great bear hugs. (At six feet three inches, he really is a big bear!) As a child, he was very calm and did not have temper issues as Mykel did. Jesse is very loving and peaceful. He does not hurt others, including plants and animals. He tends to notice quickly those in need and offers assistance. His assistance is almost always on a spiritual level, and the change in the other person is remarkable. He has little tolerance for the ego or illusions of this world. You can never put up a fake front or do false statements—he will know!

When Jesse was graduating high school, he was irritated with the graduation process. First of all, he does not like ceremonies of any kind and was having trouble with the heightened energy level and anxiety from all his classmates. He struggled most with his classmates who were to line up around him. He was irritated with the males who were putting on a show and bragging about how good they were. He found the whole thing pointless and their behaviors useless. This is where parents can help. We discussed the reasons why these children were being boastful. We helped him see the underlying issues, which increased his tolerance, although Jesse has a much more direct approach. Jesse is a master at seeing the soul for what it truly is. He deals with people differently. In a short time he can cut past all the false fronts people put up. He tells them about the true purpose of their souls. Sometimes it is overwhelming to people, but later they will come back and say, "You know, you were right, I do …" When I say to play your A game with these kids, I mean it is a requirement.

Rainbow (Doreen Virtue)

These children are being born now. Here are their characteristics:

"As crystal children are becoming adults, they give birth to *rainbow children*. These children have never lived here before and have no karma at all. They won't be born to dysfunctional families, [are] entirely fearless, ascended master-like, here for service to others, pure unconditional love and joy, here to give not to receive, and embodiment of our divinity."

Parenting these children is an incredible gift. They are meant to be with parents who have an understanding of their gifts in order not to limit these gifts. These are true gifts from God for our world. Parents should keep crystal hearts open and be real with them, even with mistakes. Parents' main focus should be to give them access to spiritual knowledge and provide an opportunity for them to continue to be open and connected. Jesse has already seen in his daughter that she is one of these children. We hope that we do our very best for her. We know the impact she will have on others.

Science has many opportunities to record and test people with these abilities. There are four brain wave frequencies: beta, alpha, theta, and delta. *Beta* waves cycle 14–30 times per second. This is consciousness, and focus is to the external world. Many people live in this state with little reflection inward and will distract themselves with the outside.

Alpha waves are from 8–13 cycles per second. This is the internal-focused mind-set associated with daydreaming, prayer, meditation, or the calmness that you feel when you are relaxing. Some of our greatest writers, poets, and musicians stay in this state while they create. This is also the state many children with attention issues are in when they are labeled as distracted and unfocused. All of us are capable of quieting the mind, focusing on a problem, and allowing the answer to come to us. This is alpha state. Meditation as a way to alpha state is harder for me at times. I can do it well while connecting in nature, floating in water, walking in the woods, or watching sunrises. Meditating in nature helps my soul ground itself and feel connected with everything.

Theta waves are 4–5 cycles per second and mean internal focus! This is deep meditation or sleep state. These are the states with close connection to God. This is the connection with our unconscious minds.

Delta waves comprise less than 4 cycles per second. This is coma, deep sleep, or a profound state of meditation. Very few people can remember events from this state of mind. For example, if you remember your dreams, you are in theta, but you will remember little from delta state.

Jesse states that we do not remember delta waves because we are gaining access to such infinite knowledge that most of the time we cannot retain such vastness. Delta is waves of pure love. It is the state of pure love that is achieved only when there are no judgments or consequences. This state can only be achieved by a few people, because it occurs in the absence of the ego or illusions.

In the mental-health field, we know that when people have hallucinations or fantasies it occurs in the neocortex. This is not activated in those who are in comas. How do those people in delta-wave state come back with stories of the other side? We do not have to die to touch the other side.

Science is beginning to prove the functions of the brain and how these "sensitive" people operate differently. It is important to understand that we are all capable of this. We can all connect and feel the One that is Everything, God, Higher Power, the Divine, the Great Spirit, etc. We can do this through prayer, meditation, finding the quiet space, and then quieting the ego's constant talk. In that space between is the connection.

When Jesus walked this earth, he came without an ego and false illusions. He stayed in the connected state with God. Therefore he was able to perform many miracles including healing. In *A Course in Miracles*, by the Foundation for Inner Peace (2008), it is stated, "Miracles occur naturally as expression of love. The real miracle is the love that inspires them. In this sense everything that comes from love is a miracle" (page 3). Healing is really about release of fear and illusions. "The miracle is the means, the atonement is the principle, and healing is the result ... All healing is essentially the release from fear" (page 23).

How do the rainbow children stay connected to the other side? How do they use their gifts to help people who are struggling to find peace, heal others, and know of events before they happen? As parents, how do we avoid responding in fear, anger, or embarrassment—and shutting down these gifts out of our own struggles? We do it with love!

We are not going to do everything right or perfect. As we've experienced, there are times when the things we've done have been more harmful than helpful. We must see all of it as a learning process, not sit in judgment. Fear is the destructive force. Fear drives our behaviors. As life events happen and we perceive them as injuries to ourselves, then we respond in fear. Not only do we judge others in that moment, but we often judge ourselves.

Forgiveness is the gift to ourselves. If we ask God to forgive us, then how can we not forgive ourselves or others? We honor God in the process of forgiveness. It liberates us. We are free indeed. It takes love to loosen the ties of fear and allow for the release of forgiveness. The greatest message all of these children are trying to communicate is, "God is love." We are loved. We are being taken care of, even through the struggles. We have these abilities to connect with God. We can help each other by lifting others up in love—and then true healing can occur for all of us.

RESOURCES

A. J. Ayres PhD, OTR; *Sensory Integration and the Child* (Los Angeles, California; Western Psychological Services, 1979)

Bonnie Arnwine; *Starting Sensory Integration Therapy* (Arlington, Texas; Future Horizon, 2005)

Carol Kranowitz; *The Out-Of-Sync Child* (New York, New York; Berkeley Publishing Group, 1998, 2005)

Cermak, Koomar, Szkult; *Making Sense of Sensory Integration* (Sensory Resources, 1998)

Doc Childre; The Institute of HeartMath; www.heartmath.org

Doreen Virtue, PhD; *Indigo, Rainbow, and Crystal Children* (Hay House, 2005)

Dr. Blair Grubb; *Syncope: Mechanisms and Management* (Wiley-Blackwell, 2005)

Dr. Wayne Dyer, James F. Twyman; *I Am Wishes Fulflled Meditation* CD (Hay House, 2012)

Frick and Richter; *Out of the Mouths of Babes* (PDP Press, 1996)

Helen Schucman and William Thetford: *A Course in Miracles* (Foundation for Inner Peace, 2008).

Jane Koomar, PhD, OTR/L, Carol Kranowitz, MA, Stacey Szklut, MS, OTR/L, Lynn Balzer-Martin, PhD, OTR/L; Elizabeth Hager, MS, OTR/L, Iris Save, MS, OTR/L; *Answers to Questions Teachers Ask about Sensory*

Integration: Forms, Checklists, and Practical Tools for Teachers (Arlington, Texas; Future Horizon, 2001)

Justin Jensen; Article: *What is Sensory Integration?*; http://prezi.com/zyglynhcwnkt/what-is-sensory-integration

Lori D'Ascenzo; www.enlightenedfeelings.com (2009)

Louise Hay; *Heal Your Body* (New York, New York; Hay House, 1978)

Louise Hay; *You can heal your life* (New York, New York; Hay House, 1984)

Lucy J Miller, Doris A Fuller; *Sensation Kids, Hope and Help for children with Sensory Processing Disorder* (Perigee Trade, 2007)

Sapolsky; *Why Zebras Don't Have Ulcers* Karen A. Smith and Karen R. Gouze; (Holt Paperback, 2004)

The Sensory Sensitive Child, Practical Solutions for Out-of-Bounds Behavior (William Morrow, 2005)

Sensory Integration Network at www.sinetwork.org

Sensory Comfort at www.sensorycomfort.com

Southpaw Enterprises at www.Southpawenterprises.com

TEACCH website for specific activities for children with autism; http://teacch.com

Terri Mauro, Sharon Cermak; *The Everything Parent's Guide to Sensory Integration Disorder* (Adams Media, 2006)

www.aromatherapy.com

www.autism.org

www.en.wikipedia.org

www.physics.org

www.science.education.nih.gov

Printed in the United States
By Bookmasters